SPEECH
FOR
THE
STAGE

EVANGELINE MACHLIN

Routledge, A Theatre Arts Book
New York   London

Copyright © 1966, 1980 by Evangeline Machlin

Paperbook published in 1992 by
Theatre Arts Book, an imprint of
Routledge
270 Madison Ave,
New York NY 10016

Transferred to Digital Printing 2009

ISBN 0-87830-120-8
ISBN 0-87830-015-5 (PB)

The Author and Publisher are grateful to the following for permission to reprint the indicated selections and photographs:

for an excerpt from "Christopher Columbus," from *The Melancholy Lute,* by Franklin P. Adams. Copyright 1962 by Dover Publications, Inc.

for Conrad Aiken's "Morning Song from Senlin" from *Collected Poems.* Copyright 1953 by Conrad Aiken. Reprinted by permission of Oxford University Press, Inc.

for Hilaire Belloc's "Jim" from *Cautionary Verses,* by Hilaire Belloc. Published 1941 by Alfred A. Knopf, Inc.

for an excerpt from Stephen Vincent Benet's "Western Star." Holt, Rinehart and Winston, Inc. Copyright 1943 by Rosemary Carr Benet, copyright renewed © 1971 by Rachel Benet Lewis, Thomas C. Benet and Stephanie Benet Mahin. Reprinted by permission of Brandt & Brandt Literary Agents, Inc.

for Robert Bly's "Clear Air of October" from *Silence in the Snowy Fields.* Copyright 1962 by Robert Bly. Wesleyan University Press. Reprinted with the author's permission.

for a selection from Rupert Brooke's "Grantchester" from *The Collected Poems of Rupert Brooke.* With the permission of the publishers, Dodd, Mead & Company, Inc.

for thirty-five lines from G. K. Chesterton's "Lepanto." Reprinted by permission of Dodd, Mead & Company, Inc. from *The Collected Poems of G. K. Chesterton.* Copyright 1932 by Dodd, Mead & Company, Inc. Copyright renewed 1959 by Oliver Chesterton.

Publisher's Note
The publisher has gone to great lengths to ensure the quality of this reprint but points out that some imperfections in the original may be apparent.

Foreword: to the Student

I have an enormous respect for
technique, and a great impatience
for people who are not prepared.

HAROLD PRINCE
New York Times, January 20, 1980

THIS FOREWORD GIVES you a foretaste of this book. In it you will be offered a direct, straightforward approach to speech training, appropriate to this age of satellite communications and computerized speech. The book asks you to think of speech in scientific terms, as a physical entity, a series of sound waves, a train of pressure pulses, sent out by you through the air to all ears within reach. These waves you create at the vocal cords, modify in the mouth, and send out at the speed of sound. No freeing of the voice is needed; like Elsa the lioness, it was born free. Open your mouth and let it out. Do make waves!

To understand the nature of theatre speech, analyze the speech act from your point of view, the actor's. Notice the fourfold sequence. Part One is a *proposal* in the brain. Each time you speak, you propose and decide in a flash of time what you wish to say. Part Two is a *process*, the means by which you speak. Down from the brain come motor messages to the muscles of the vocal tract, making them act on the exhaling air in ways you learned in infancy when you discovered how to talk. These actions result in Part Three, a *product*, the sound waves of speech. Part Four is a *printout;* the waves reach your listener's eardrum and beat on it so that it vibrates in phase with them. These vibrations, transformed into electrochemical impulses, rush up the nerve of hearing to the brain. The brain, in a way not yet fully understood, prints them out on the consciousness as words and sentences. The chain of speech communication is complete.

The playwright has proposed the words you will speak; the audience does the hearing and understanding. Therefore, as an actor, you are concerned only with Part Two of this sequence, the process. The process is all-important; it controls the product. The product in your case is speech for the stage—pleasant to hear, easy to understand, compelling to follow.

If the speech is harsh or slurred—if, so to speak, there are imperfections in the product—you exercise over it what engineers call "quality control." You monitor your speech, partly by feel, but chiefly by ear, catching errors as they occur. The ear becomes to the actor what the eye is to the dancer, who monitors his movements in the mirror at the dance studio. He *sees* his failings; you *hear* yours. Both of you, seeking excellence, self-correct. What begins as a craft will end as an art.

The dancer practices the muscular acts of dance till he achieves absolute control. He wants a perfect product, flawless performance. So do you. Like him, you practice for perfection. It is not your moods but your movements that you change to make your speech better. Come to the task as you would to a swimming lesson, or a typing lesson, or anything that requires smooth coordination of many muscle groups. Let us suppose that you already swim or type or play after a fashion. But you do not do these things well. You can *learn* to do them smoothly, effortlessly, and ultimately with mastery. You can also learn to master the techniques of speech for the stage.

"Practicing is the most satisfying work I have," said Yehudi Menuhin recently. Let it be so for you. This book will tell you in simple, concrete terms what and how to practice. No pseudo-psychological approaches to your speech problems will be made. No bewildering commands (like one that originated in England—"I want to hear you, not your voice") will confuse you.

Remember, though, that you learn speech techniques to forget them. Good habits, once established, sink from the conscious level to the reflex level, needing no more direction from you. When this happens with your speech, clear phonation, firm articulation, and flexible inflections will always characterize it. On the stage you will never have to think about it. Like a well-trained servant, your voice will obey your slightest command. You, the actor, can give your entire consciousness to creating your role.

Accordingly, this book begins and ends with work. The Actor's Daily Routine is on the front endpaper, the Actor's Warm-Up Exercises on the last. The latter, a short but useful series, is one which you should invariably undertake whenever you are about to use your speech in a situation calling for projection. It warms up the vocal tract, letting you speak with range and richness from the first syllable on. Make this warm-up your habit before each rehearsal and performance.

The Actor's Practice Routine, a complete set of speech-building exercises, is on the front endpaper for ready reference. Make a habit of following it during your daily practice periods. It is planned to serve as the basis of the regular, long-continued practice of speech techniques which will be the foundation of lifelong power and flexibility in your speech. Each unit in the Routine lends itself to endless variations, so that your practice may be freshened from day to day and from month to month. The drills in Unit 4, for example, may revolve around new sequences and new groups of vowels and consonants. The articulation and the reading-aloud units may draw on the whole world of English literature, prose and poetry as well as drama.

The Actor's Warm-Up Exercises are self-explanatory and may be used immediately. The Practice Routine needs to be undertaken gradually, as you master the theory underlying each unit of the Practice Routine. The book is designed to promote the simultaneous growth of a broad spectrum of speech skills. Chapters 1, 2, 3, and 4 on listening, projection, and the mechanics of the vocal tract, are fundamental to all speech study. Chapters 5 through 9 present the theory and technique of breath control, tone production, articulation, and speech variety. Chapters 10, 11, and 12 deal with Shakespearean speech, dialect speech, and speech for sight-reading and auditions.

Begin with a rapid reading of Chapters 1, 2, 3, and 4. Plan on a long-range program of work on listening and projection with reference as needed to the mechanics of speech. Study Chapters 5 and 6 and undertake Units 1, 2, and 3 of the Practice Routine thereafter. Add Unit 4 when Chapter 7 has been mastered, and so on. Use the Routine daily, until you can work through all the units. Reserve work on the later chapters until you have some competence in the basic techniques. Meanwhile, use the Warm-Up Exercises as needed, for readying of your speech for quick action.

The Practice Routine, when fully developed, will require from fifteen minutes to an hour to complete. Never spend less time than the minimum, rarely more than the maximum, in practice. Speech technique is like dance technique; being the work of muscles, it benefits most from regular practice in sufficient amounts. Plan to work at a fixed time in a specific place, so that habit may help your resolution not to miss a day of routine speech practice.

Your early objective should be to acquire both a habitual method of work and a repertoire of exercises to work with. By varying the exercises as suggested and by inventing new ones, you will renew your interest and propel yourself to vigorous effort. Regard the development of your speech as never completed, always progressing towards greater ease and brilliance. Daily practice is a present means to a future end that expands and changes even as it is achieved—the realization of the full potentiality of your speech for the stage.

For their help in preparing this book I want to thank Bob Bruyr for making many of the drawings, Anthony J. Moscatel and C. John MacFarlane who took the photographs not otherwise acknowledged, and, above all others, my husband Stuart Machlin, for his constant help.

EVANGELINE MACHLIN,
Professor Emerita,
Division of Theatre,
School for the Arts,
Boston University

Contents

LIST OF PLATES

LIST OF FIGURES

1 | ↜
Listening and Learning:
Speech Appreciation

Of all wonders, none is more wonderful than man,
Who has learned the art of speech.

SOPHOCLES

THE PURPOSE of this book is to help you to develop good speech for the stage. It begins with listening, which is the basis of all speech acquisition. When you were an infant, you listened for almost a year before you began to speak. Your first random efforts at speech imitation were sometimes successful, sometimes unsuccessful. The successful ones were rewarded with response and commendation, and your hearing prompted you to repeat them correctly. Now that you intend to retrain your speech for the stage, you must once more begin by listening.

All human speech involves simultaneous hearing and speaking, with the ear as the feedback system for the brain. If you make a mistake when you speak, perhaps mispronouncing a word or transposing sounds as did the Englishman who cried, "How pleasant to ride a well-boiled icicle!" your ear will tell you so at once. This corrective return is all-important for you as an actor. Your ear must be a good corrector. It must warn you not only of gross faults in your speech but also of less obvious ones like low volume, dull tone, or slurred articulation. Learning this fine kind of discrimination through the ear is a vital part of your speech training. It is accomplished by listening to speech as a musician listens to music, for pleasure, pure and unadulterated, and also for profit. The musician profits through analyzing what he hears, noting the dynamics of the performance, studying the tone quality, observing the pianissimo and fortissimo passages, and appraising the skill of the performer. A player himself, the musician will presently apply this critical analysis to his own technique with great benefit. Similarly, your ear will gradually acquire the same kind of skill in analyzing speaking voices, especially those of actors. Listening closely and often to live actors and to records of the best speaking voices of this century, you will gain a thorough knowledge of what speech qualities you need most—breath control, resonant tone, clear articulation, and variety of pitch, speed, and stress.

This chapter has been placed first in this book because the training of the actor's ear should underlie and accompany all his other work. Only when your ear is sharpened by disciplined listening to catch such tiny sounds as the intake of John Gielgud's breath, for example, before a great cry in one of his Shakespearean recordings will you realize exactly what you must accomplish in breath control to achieve a like perfection. It is the same with the other techniques of speech. "Hearing and obedience!" as the slave used to say to the Caliph in *Arabian Nights,* is an excellent attitude for your voice to take towards your ear. You should begin your listening program now, and hereafter organize it around your studies in each chapter, listening especially to tone quality when you are working on Chapter 7, to the articulation of sounds with Chapter 8, and so on.

Attend the legitimate theatre as much as possible. If you have to be content with a seat far from the stage, you can make a virtue of necessity by noting what kind of voices are easiest to hear from a long distance. See a play more than once, and as you get familiar with the script, watch the actors' speech as well as listen to it. Howard Taubman has pointed out in the New York *Times* that many American actors are desperately handicapped by bad speech habits. You should judge for yourself whether or not you agree with him.

The speech of actors in movies, on television, and increasingly on records and retakes has been so much regulated in electronic reproduction that it is less valuable for you than actors' live speech. Such speech often has to contend with poor theatre acoustics, fatigue, and all the other hazards of the stage. If it is successful, you will gain by observing and learning from it. Yet television speech can yield you profit too, if you turn off the sound from time to time and watch only the mouth movements of the speakers. Suddenly the role of these movements in shaping the sounds of speech becomes exceedingly clear. The agility of tongue, lip, and jaw movements, if the actor's speech is well articulated, should be most instructive for you.

For your listening studies, you will need access to a record player, a tape recorder, and a supply of speech records, primarily of recorded plays. Your school or college may possess sound equipment and a good library of speech recordings. If it does not, you should begin to make your own record collection, following three principles of selection. First, choose chiefly voices of good American actors. Second, choose plays (or prose or poetry) of literary merit. Third, in general, choose a play recording that was made by the original cast of a successful production of the play during its run. Such recordings reflect the life and fire of the real performance, the timing that audience reaction evoked, the pitch builds evolved through many rehearsals, the pauses, and the bursts of speed, everything that may make your listening experience parallel to one in the live theatre. Studio recordings made by a group of actors called together to read a play sometimes lack these qualities. These recordings are less suitable for your purpose.

You should listen to readings of poetry and prose, as well as to plays. Listening to a theatre voice in short units, reading poems or prose beautifully or comically (as the case may be), is often very rewarding. Choose by the actor or actress, not by the selection.

Listen chiefly to American actors and actresses. There are plenty of good ones. At this writing the recorded voices of Jane Alexander, Mildred Dunnock, Tammy Grimes, Julie Harris, Katharine Hepburn, and Lee Remick are available, among others. Long-established professional actors like Ed Begley, Lee J. Cobb, Joseph Cotten, Henry Fonda, Bert Lahr, E. G. Marshall, and Zero Mostel have also been recorded. The original cast recording of *For Colored Girls Who Have Considered Suicide When the Rainbow Is Enuf* features many interesting women's voices. That of *The Boys in the Band* includes a variety of men's voices.

English actors' voices do not now sound as clipped as they used to. No longer is "received speech"—the speech of the British aristocracy—demanded on the English stage. Today there is much back-and-forth travel of actors between London and New York, and we are used to mixed casts of British and American actors in the same play. A transatlantic modified British is what we hear. For this reason, you should listen to the best actresses—Claire Bloom, Maggie Smith, Vanessa Redgrave, Irene Worth— and the best actors—Albert Finney, Alec McGowen, Cyril Ritchard, Paul Scofield.

Do not overlook the very greatest voices, those of the British stage personalities of this century who were honored with titles by the Queen. Among the women, try to hear Dame Edith Evans, Dame Flora Robson, and especially Dame Sybil Thorndike—she of whom Shaw cried, as he met her, "Here at last is my Saint Joan! I can produce the play!" In her old age, Miss Thorndike confessed that she still kept up her voice exercises. She was a grande dame of the theatre: People said, "Sybil swept into her eighties like a ship in full sail!" As for men, try to hear Sir John Gielgud, Lord Olivier, Sir Michael Redgrave, and Sir Ralph Richardson. Many of the great Shakespeare performances made in the fifties and sixties by these and other actors are no longer listed in the catalogues, but your school library may still have them. Check a recent catalogue for others.

In earlier decades some play productions in America and Canada were theatrical events of the century. You need not miss these merely because you were not born then. Those that (happily) are still available you should hear. One was the Stratford, Ontario, production in the fifties of Sophocles' *Oedipus Rex,* with the great Canadian actor Douglas Campbell in the leading role. The climactic moment of the play was the dreadful scream Campbell gave at the moment he discovered his true identity. It was so harrowing a moment of catharsis that in 1980 Harold Prince declared he still remembered the scream. Another masterpiece of the theatre was the production of Arthur Miller's *Death of a Salesman* with Mildred Dunnock and Lee J. Cobb. Hear it and understand the compelling nature of Miller's best play performed by incomparable artists. Equally unforgettable was Paul Robeson's *Othello* in the forties, his artistry lost to us in all but this recording. With him were his near-equals: José Ferrer as Iago, the young Uta Hagen as Desdemona (later to earn plaudits in a contrasting role as Martha of *Who's Afraid of Virginia Woolf?*), and Margaret Webster, the great English actress-director, as Emilia. Pay close attention to the jealousy scene between Robeson and Ferrer, particularly when the latter, with superb finesse expressed in the most subtle inflections, hints at Desdemona's infidelity with Cassio:

OTHELLO: (*Speaking of* CASSIO) Is he not honest?
IAGO: My lord, for aught I know.
OTHELLO: What dost thou think?

IAGO:	Think, my lord?	
OTHELLO:		Think, my lord!

By heaven, he echoes me
As if there were some monster in his thought
Too hideous to be shown.

The time to listen to a Shakespeare play in its entirety is when you are cast in one. If it is *Hamlet* or *King Lear*, listen to all the *Hamlet* and *Lear* recordings your library has. You will understand your lines better—and find your own interpretation of them more rapidly—when you have heard how others solved the problems of speaking Shakespearean blank verse. Study the way different actors handle the run-on lines, the long speeches. What was the speed? What was the pitch-range? Can you, with your native American, match the crisp consonants the British use? With practice you can.

Aside from plays, there are three recordings of Shakespeare that outshine the rest. The first and the best of these is *Homage to Shakespeare*. It was produced in England in 1964, Shakespeare's quadricentennial year. To do him honor, all the greatest actors contributed readings, so that we have on one record the best work of the best. On it you may hear Olivier, Gielgud, Worth, Evans and others, each reading passages from different plays—another virtue of this recording. Especially distinctive is Olivier's Othello; he chose not a violent speech but a calm one. Beginning with "Her father lov'd me," he explains to the Duke in quiet, low-pitched tones how Desdemona fell in love with him simply by hearing him talk with her father. Any actor wanting to learn what has well been called "the emphasis of restraint" should listen to it.°

The second great Shakespearean record, one that also uses material from many plays, is Sir John Gielgud's *Ages of Man,* called "a masterpiece" by the *Times* when it was produced. To see and hear Gielgud perform one splendid

° Olivier, then at the height of his career, did not hesitate to undertake six weeks of study with a speech teacher before the production to lower his pitch for the role.

sequence after another was a profound experience. He was on the stage alone throughout; yet when he impersonated Lear in the scene with the murdered Cordelia, his cry "O, ye are men of stone!" to those supposedly present seemed to fill the stage with actors. Nor was there a dry eye in the sophisticated New York audience at the lines

> No, no, no life! . . .
> Thou'lt come no more,
> Never, never, never, never, never . . .

Finally, listen to John Barrymore, whose greatest Shakespearean soliloquies have been preserved by AudioRarities. His opening speech as Richard III, his "Ah vengeance!" monologue as Hamlet, will change any room into a theatre as you listen. Certainly the style is that of a past day, but it is spellbinding, even though melodramatic.

If you feel you have the comic gift, listen to the voices of artists like Hermione Gingold, whose madcap recordings create as hilarious a mood as did her stage appearances. The deliveries of Victor Borge, Flip Wilson, and Stan Freberg will let you hear timing, the essence of comedy. From the long list of humorous recordings available, choose the voices you know from the stage or TV. Concentrate on and learn from your favorites. Comedy is a great and rare gift, and an individual style is part of it.

You may also listen to theatre voices reading poetry and prose. Later in this book, you will be asked to try reading aloud to young children. Study recordings made for children by good actors. *Silver Pennies*, with Cyril Ritchard and Claire Bloom reading, is among the best. The book *Silver Pennies* is an outstanding collection of poems for children, some simple, some fantastical, like

> The moon? It is a griffin's egg
> Hatching to-morrow night . . .

Children love best uninhibited readings, and these, along with Boris Karloff's inimitable recording of Kipling's *Just-So*

Stories, will show you how an actor's voice may range tremendously in pitch, in stress, in speed, and in the use of pause, with the attention-getting result the actor needs.

Do not neglect recordings of the untrained voice. You can learn much about the differences between the trained and untrained voice, for example, by listening to the voices of poets reading their own poetry. Listen to the young Sylvia Plath, then to the older Marianne Moore. Listen to Robert Frost's gritty voice reading his poems in his old age, still able to hold an audience.

Documentary recordings, of which a growing number are becoming available, supply listening studies of several kinds. One is the study of a public figure's speaking voice to discover how character is expressed and felt in vocal elements. Another is the study of authentic regionalisms. A third is the study of how speech behaves under strain. An album especially rich in these elements is Volume I of *I Can Hear It Now,* a record of the World War II years and those just following. It presents the great war speeches of Roosevelt and Churchill and snatches of public addresses of Hitler and Mussolini; you will notice the remarkable contrast between the hysterical shrillness of the latter two and the controlled eloquence of the former pair. The album also includes American voices from different backgrounds, each with its distinctive regional variants: Fiorello La-Guardia's, Will Rogers', and Alfred Smith's, among others. It presents samples of historical news broadcasts, such as the one in which an announcer's lively tones, describing the safe arrival of a dirigible at its mooring-mast after a trans-Atlantic crossing, suddenly change to an anguished scream as he sees it fall in flames before his eyes. Another kind of speech change significant for you as an actor is that heard in the documentary *Hearings of the Un-American Activities Committee.* Here are actual recordings of the proceedings of Senator Joseph McCarthy's Committee, examining witnesses to determine if they had Communist associations. Extreme hesitation and weak fading tone characterize the speech of some witnesses, while that of others expresses indignation, anger, and contempt. You may wish to compare this genuine document with a satire based upon it, a radio drama originating in Canada and subsequently released here as a record called *The Investigator*. The actor who plays the investigator does a brilliant imitation of Senator McCarthy's voice. At a time when the Senator's voice and methods were familiar to everyone, the writer saw a sidewalk crowd collecting on Sixth Avenue when this record was played over the loudspeaker of a record shop. Gradually, it became clear that the voice was not really the Senator's but an actor impersonating him. The crowd, realizing this, reacted with astonishment.

When you come to study articulation, enjoy a record, *The Tongue Twisters,* on which are arranged in alphabetical order by initial letter posers like "Sister Susie," she who sewed shirts for soldiers, and "Shrewd Simon Short." You can lip along with George Irving, trying to equal his comic clarity. The label and number for this and all other records mentioned in this chapter are listed beginning on page 216.

The ability to imitate a particular kind of speech or pick up a dialect is an extra skill possessed by some actors. Chapter 11 of this book briefly describes how to do this. A full description of the methods to use, with cassettes of twenty selected dialects, is found in the author's *Dialects for the Stage* (Theatre Arts Books, 1973).

Speech appreciation exercise

1. Each week of the semester, choose a recording by an actor or actress or group of players from the record list beginning on page 216, or from your school library's collection. Listen to one voice on the record especially, until you become familiar with it. Write a short comment on why you think it is a good (or a poor) theatre voice.

2 | ∿
Listening and Learning:
Speech Analysis

In speech . . . corrective return comes by ear.
E. LLOYD DUBRUL, *Theory of the Evolution of Behavior*

BESIDES THE general kinds of listening described in Chapter 1, you should undertake two special kinds. The first is organized around the separate techniques of stage speech as presented in this book. Each of Chapters 1 through 11 deals with a technique and is followed by exercises for developing that technique. (In Chapter 12, the exercises for the technique are incorporated in the text of the chapter.) One of these exercises is a listening assignment in the first kind of listening. It is designed to teach your ear to recognize certain speech qualities so that it may properly guide your efforts to develop them yourself. The second kind of listening teaches you a method of analyzing a speaking voice by isolating and judging each of its qualities to the best of your ability. You are required to back up your estimate in each case by selecting and listing the word or phrase in which you hear that quality illustrated. You are also asked to summarize the effect the speech has upon you as a listener. An analysis form lists the qualities in the order in which they are presented in this book, with spaces for checking their presence or absence and for listing illustrative words. Directions for using the form, and one blank form appears at the end of this chapter.

Your ultimate objective will be to analyze successfully your own recorded speech. Your first attempt, however, should be with the speech of another. The easiest speech to analyze is one in which glaring faults are present. Any ear can recognize a nasal twang, hoarseness, or a pronunciation like "toid" for "third." If possible, record such speech for analysis. Or choose from a library a documentary recording of a voice you consider uncultivated. *New York 19*, a record under the Folkways label, was made from candid recordings taken in Postal District 19 of New York City. It is one of the few available records in which you can hear the neighborhood speech of the uneducated. One of the voices heard on it may do for your first analysis. Analyze it step by step, following the directions. A friend or fellow-student may analyze it, too, so that you may compare notes as to what you found.

A second analysis may be made from the speech of an educated person who has not had speech training, using the recorded voices of poets and authors. All the more because they are untrained, these voices suggest the writer's personality. Do not expect to find them free of speech faults. Literary men are not always public speakers, just as composers of music are not always concert performers. Your business as a learning listener is not to reject the voice of the poet or author because it is untrained but to note that, for all its underlying sympathy with and understanding of the material, it may sound flat and monotonous in comparison with the trained voice of an actor. You should analyze several such voices, and draw your own conclusions.

You are now ready to analyze your own speech. Record it at the very beginning of your training, and make an analysis of it immediately thereafter to the best of your ability. The process will help you to discover the weakest points in your speech at present. The recording will act as a yardstick by which to measure improvement in future recordings of your voice. It should be of yourself in conversation, not reading, so that you will be less able to mask your own speech faults.

Prepare for this important first recording by experimenting with your microphone, your tape recorder's controls, and the place in which you will speak, so as to obtain the conditions which result in the most natural reproduction of your speech. Record at 7½ rpm for greatest fidelity. Set the index counter at zero. Measure the distance from the microphone to where you will sit. Make a note of this, and also note the exact settings of the controls. (These precautions are taken so that later recordings may be made under the same conditions as the first.) Since you are going to record conversation, you will need someone to converse with. Your speech teacher or a helpful friend who will act as teacher may help you. He should sit opposite you at a natural distance for conversation.

Begin your recording by stating your name, the date, and your place of birth. This last information is important with regard to possible regionalisms in your speech. Then state your chosen topic simply: "I am going to talk about an unusual movie I saw last night." Any topic in which you have a lively interest will serve. To start off naturally, enter into conversation about it with your teacher or friend, who may ask you questions if needed to keep you going. As soon as possible, carry the talk by yourself, continuing without interruption for about a minute. Note the point on the index counter at which you finish.

Play back the recording, and at once note down your first impressions of your voice, both its strong and weak points. Be as objective as possible. Above all, do not reject your voice in despair because it has faults. Your teacher or friend may help you in pointing out good qualities as well as defects you have missed. Now analyze your speech on the form provided, again with your teacher's help. When the analysis is finished, the tape should be reserved, no further additions being made to it for some time. Nor should you listen to it again until later.

Study your analysis carefully, and note in what area your worst speech faults are. As you work through this book, developing each technique in turn, you will presently arrive at the remedial work for one of your particular faults. Adjust your daily practice period to allow extra time for this special work, but do not let it take up more than one-third of the whole period. Do not be in a hurry to leave any remedial work. If, for example, your articulation tends to be slurred, you should stay with the corrective work until all your consonants are clearly made in the exercise routine, in reading aloud, and in conversation. Deal with each of your faults in turn in the same way.

You may use a tape recorder for the correction of your speech faults during your practice periods if you are careful to limit its use to this purpose only. Long continuous recordings of your own voice will not help you. You may only be practicing your own errors! It is more effective to record small samples of your voice working at various speech techniques that need improvement. If, for instance, your tone is poor, short phrases for resonance development as given in Chapter 5 may be recorded, listened to, re-recorded, and listened to again. Then you may make a definite attempt to enrich this resonance with each repetition. Keep these practice units in a sequence, so that when you play them back you may judge whether you are improving. Keep the same small-unit approach in using the tape recorder with all the exercises.

At the end of perhaps eight months to a year of daily practice, you may make a second conversational recording following the first. Be careful that all the conditions are exactly as they were the first time. Do not play the first recording back to yourself until the second is made.

Begin at the point noted on the index counter at the end of the first one. You alone should speak this time, beginning with the date, and launching into talk on the old topic or on a new one, as you prefer.

Now play the tape through from first to last, your voice in September followed by your voice in May or the next September. The tape recorder cannot lie, and at once you will discover how and to what degree your speech has improved. If you have worked faithfully, the contrast between the two recordings may amaze and delight you. Often there is a great change in the power and resonance of the speech tone after a year's work. Other areas may also have improved.

This improvement should spur you to continue, making another recording at the end of a second year of training. You may expect further gains, especially in articulation and in variety, speech techniques which usually take time to develop. A recording made at the end of a third year's work should show your speech easy and full, all the techniques developed to a point where they are readily available both for your everyday speech and for your speech on the stage.

As with any skill, when you become a proficient speaker, you will enjoy all the more proficiency in the speech of others. The art of listening will deepen your enjoyment of good speech wherever you hear it, and you will take special pleasure in hearing the power, beauty, and clarity of stage speech. Your speech, too, will gradually develop these qualities. Among them, power, or the ability to project one's speech, is acquired most readily because it is naturally present in speech. The technique by which you may develop it to the full for stage use is the subject of the next chapter.

Speech Analysis Exercises

1. The haiku below are mini-poems—sensitive, witty, conversational. Read them aloud, enjoying them, and when you feel familiar with them, record them. Have a friend do the same; thereafter, each may analyze the other's readings, using the form overleaf.

AFTER THE GENTLE POET KOBAYASHI ISSA

New Year's morning— ·
everything is in blossom!
I feel about average.

A huge frog and I
staring at each other,
neither of us moves.

Asked how old he was,
the boy in the new kimono
stretched out all five fingers.

Don't worry, spiders,
I keep house
casually.

Hell:

Bright autumn moon
pond snails crying
in the saucepan.

ROBERT HASS

2. Analyze recorded voices: Robert Frost's on *Robert Frost in Recital* and any voice on *Into the Storm—The Coming of War, 1939*. See p. 219.

SPEECH ANALYSIS FORM

Speech of (name) _____ Analyzer's name _____ Date _____
Speech material (check one): Conversation _____ Reading _____ Record _____
Record label and number _____ Record title _____

Directions: Listen repeatedly to the speech to be analyzed. Concentrate on each of the speech qualities listed in turn. For each quality, underline the descriptive term or terms that apply. Opposite the term, write the words or words of the speaker in which you heard this quality. For the negative qualities in 7 and 8, write the error words first in spelling, then in IPA, to show the errors.

Positive Speech Qualities	Negative Speech Qualities

1. Relaxation

Speech is relaxed _____
Speech is rhythmic, fluent _____

Speech is tense _____
Speech is nonrhythmic, jerky _____

2. Breath Control

Inhalations:
　Silent or barely audible _____
　Well-timed _____

Inhalations:
　Noisy _____
　Poorly-timed _____

3. Resonance

Tone:
　Resonant _____
　Clear _____
　Mouth-produced _____
　Full _____

Tone:
　Strident _____
　Hoarse _____
　Nasal _____
　Breathy _____

4. Pitch

Pitch:
　Free-ranging _____
　Inflections meaningful _____
　_____
　_____
　_____
　_____

Pitch:
　Monotonous _____
　Too high _____
　Too low _____
　End-dropped _____
　Patterned (show pattern with
　　dots) _____

5. Rate

Rate:
　Appropriate _____
　_____
　_____

Rate:
　Unvaried _____
　Too fast _____
　Too slow _____

6. Stress

Stresses:
　Meaningful _____
　_____

Stresses:
　Too heavy _____
　Too light _____

7. Articulation

Articulation:
　Sharp, brilliant _____
　_____

Articulation:
　Slurred _____
　_____

8. Pronunciation

Pronunciation:
　Standard American _____
　Standard Canadian _____
　Standard British _____

Pronunciation:
　Regional or dialectal (name
　　region or dialect) _____
　_____
　Substandard _____

SUMMARY: Effectiveness of total speech _____

Reprinted from Evangeline Machlin, Speech for the Stage, Theatre Arts Books

3 | ⟋

Projecting Your Speech

Shout round me, let me hear thy shouts, thou happy
Shepherd-Boy!
WORDSWORTH, *Ode on the Intimations of Immortality*

THE PROJECTION OF speech on the stage is exactly what the
word suggests: the vigorous throwing out of the sounds
that make up the words you speak. Such projection is
a natural act. People exclaim at the top of their voices
when happy or when horrified. The cheerleaders at a
football game (Plate I) hail their team's success with
shouts of joy. Their action in creating these loud shouts
is plain to see. They open their mouths wide and let the
sounds out freely. You, too, as an actor, need loud tones.
Natural loudness is quite easy to achieve, and this chapter presents a way of getting it into your speech at once.
Improvement in the quality of your speech is harder to
achieve and takes longer. Chapters 5, 6, 7, 8, and 9 will
deal with various aspects of beauty and clarity in speech
and explain how to develop them, but simple projection
of the speech you now have can be achieved at once.

All creatures with vocal tracts like ours open their
mouths wide instinctively when they wish their cries
to be heard at a distance. Cats meow and dogs bark with
wide-stretched jaws. A baby screams with his mouth as
wide open as any cheerleader's. His mother will tell you
how well he projects his cry—through walls and closed
doors, from upstairs to downstairs, or from indoors to out.

PLATE I.

In childhood your own speech was probably loud and clear. A happy pre-schooler laughs and shouts at the top of his voice, and so, no doubt, did you.

Since then, however, you have spent twelve years in school. Through most of your hours there an unnatural silence was imposed upon you. Most of your teachers believed in the old adage "Silence is golden." They taught you to read and write much more than to argue and discuss. Not only shades of the prison-house but its silences, too, began to close about the growing child. Such oral work as you did do in school was probably carried on in restrained tones. You stopped opening your mouth well when you spoke. Later, your evenings during high school years were largely spent preparing written, not oral, homework. No wonder your speech suffered! As a high school graduate you might have emerged with a well-trained mind and even a physically fit body, but you probably finished with speech that was de-energized, unresonant, lazy-lipped, and tight-jawed.

Now you must correct these bad habits. You must

learn again to open your mouth well when you speak and project as you did when a child. Remember that the habit of low-level speech is in your ear as well as in your mouth. Your ear is not accustomed to hearing yourself make strong, vigorous sounds when you speak. When you begin to project again, your ear may insist for some time that this louder speech is inappropriate. This will be especially true when you are engaged in a quiet scene on the stage. Hushed tones seem always to be right for either tender or sinister speech exchanges. Yet, if you follow the dictates of your instinct and keep your voice low, the members of the audience up in the top balcony will be unable to hear you. Even in intimate scenes, you must open your mouth and let the sound out if it is to travel all through the theatre.

It may help you to remember that in opening your mouth to project, you are not so much learning to do something properly as unlearning a wrong habit which was superimposed by authority. The freedom of your speech was blocked by long silences that prevented you from exercising it and keeping it strong and athletic. Now you must remove the blocks, let down the barriers, and strengthen the movements. Your own natural, unhindered speech is large enough for the stage. Speak freely, open your mouth wide, and let your speech tones ring out almost as in song. This increase in volume will be immediate and significant.

The effect need not be one of shouting. Opening the mouth improves the resonance of the tone as well as increasing its volume, a fact that will be brought out in the following chapters. You can test it at once by a simple speech experiment. Speak the sentence, "*I will open my mouth wide, and try at the same time to speak quietly.*" Suit the action to the words, stretching your mouth especially wide for each of the six *i* sounds in the sentence, but reducing the energy with which you speak. You will find that the words *I, my, wide, try, time,* and *quietly* tend to ring out loudly as do all the vowels and diphthongs from a well-opened mouth.

Open vowels in projected speech are matched by firmly closed consonants. It is obvious that swinging the jaw open wide for the *i* in *time* means that it must travel farther to close the lips for the *m* which follows. The action must accordingly be brisk both ways. As all vowels are made with various open positions of the mouth, so all consonants are made with constrictions of different shapes and sizes. The alignment of the mouth for each will be fully explained in Chapter 8, which deals with articulation. In the meantime, however, as you accustom yourself to the wide openings of projected vowels, you should also practice the firm closures of projected consonants. Be especially careful with final consonants, particularly if they occur at the end of an unaccented syllable. Final *l*'s and *n*'s in words like *feeble, double, common, broken,* etc., tend to be laxly closed. Even in enlarged speech they may sound like *feebuh, doubuh, commuh, brokuh.* Pronounce them with a firm pressure of the tongue on the hard palate. Experiment with a sentence like "He was too feeble to be able to fasten the broken button," and hear what a difference a good closure makes to the intelligibility of words ending in *l* and *n*.

Opening and closing the mouth well to project speech is a principle based on both the nature of sound and the acoustics of theatres. Speech sounds, like all sounds, are pressure disturbances. The motive power for the disturbance is the upcoming stream of air from the lungs. The source of the disturbance is the vibration of the vocal cords, opening and closing as the air forces its way between them. In so doing, they start sound waves, pulses of alternating rarefaction and condensation of air molecules, that move out into all the open spaces to which they are admitted. They act somewhat like water pouring from an opening under pressure. If the opening is a main hydrant rather than a faucet, much more water will pour out. It is so with the sound waves coming out of your mouth. Barely open your lips, and you will cut down the volume of the escaping sound wave very much. Open them wide, and much more of it will emerge.

Consider also what happens to the sound waves of speech as they travel across the theatre. Each sound is a pressure disturbance of a certain shape and force. It moves through the air as a ripple moves out in an expanding circle from the splash made when a stone is thrown into a pond. The water itself does not travel across the pond. The wave, a small backward-and-forward motion, travels across its surface. Each sound wave likewise travels through the air, compressing the molecules ahead of it and rarefying those behind it. Its ripples do not move horizontally, however. They travel as expanding spheres. Each sphere-shaped pulse expands with the enormous speed of sound, 1,130 feet per second, like a jet plane breaking the sound barrier. Thus, in a flash of time the words you speak on the stage shoot out as pressure waves in all directions to the extremities of the theatre. The farther they go, the more spread out they become and the weaker and fainter grows each resulting sound as its energy is extended over larger and larger spheres. You will realize how great the spread is if you recall the area of a sphere in relation to its diameter. At 12 feet from your mouth, the energy of each sound you speak is spread out over a sphere with a surface of 65,000 square inches, the size of a large room. At 60 feet away, this area has increased to more than an acre! A pair of listening ears at the back of a theatre will receive only an incredibly small part of the original sound energy with which you spoke. Thus, you had better let out as much of it as you can by opening your mouth wide as you speak.

Finally, consider the effect of acoustics upon the sound waves you make. Sounds reverberate in an empty hall. They bounce back from every hard surface they strike, recrossing the original waves, which they can pass through without interacting with them. The listener sitting in the middle of an empty hall will hear not only the sound waves that first left your mouth, but also those that are reflected from the walls, the ceiling and the floor. The reflected waves will reach his ear a fraction of a second later than the original ones, tending both to mask and to distort them. This distortion effect is called the "reverberation time" of the hall. It is sometimes so great that the words of the speaker cannot be understood, although their sound can be heard.

By the same token, it is much easier for you to project your speech in a full house. Any absorbent material—draperies, upholstery, peoples' clothes and bodies—all absorb reflected sound waves and permit the original ones to dominate. If these absorbent materials are less because the house is half-full or, worse still, nearly empty, you must project as vigorously as you can, to make up for the distortion that may occur. If you are in an outdoor theatre it may well be shaped like a Greek amphitheatre, with a circling hillside, on which tiers of seats have been set up, around the stage. Even Greek actors, however, used megaphones built into their masks as amplifiers. The megaphone mouth perpetually stood wide open and must have served as a fine aid to projection!

Fortunately for modern actors, loudspeaker systems accomplish this in most outdoor theatres. You will be well advised, none the less, to practice continually with a well-opened mouth so that you may be heard in any circumstances, whatever the acoustics of the place you act in.

Good acoustics in the theatre seems to be sometimes a matter of design, sometimes a matter of the fashion of the times, and sometimes a matter of luck. In Shakespeare's little Globe, the stage projected halfway down the arena. The galleries around were the reverse of what we now have in balconies. The higher they were, the further forward they projected. They must have collected the sound waves like the shell over an outdoor orchestra's platform. In Canada's Festival Theatre at Stratford, Ontario, the circular shape of the original tent was retained in the permanent theatre. It was built around an open hexagonal stage serving it like Mr. Looking-All-Ways. This arrangement proved to be acoustically admirable. Most university theatres in the United States and Canada boast fine modern theatre auditoriums, indoors and sometimes out. But few could excel acoustically Boston University's old theatre, built in 1925 as the Jewett Repertory Theatre, with its high, ornate ceiling, steep balcony, and overstuffed upholstered seats, the pride of

PLATE II. Festival Theater at Stratford, Ontario

the showy 'twenties. In Pitlochry, Scotland, by contrast, is a small Festival theatre that owes its near-perfect acoustics to good Scotch thrift. The visitor hears the softest word perfectly in the farthest seat and wonders if the fabric walls and billowing slipper-satin ceiling were included for acoustical reasons. Later he learns that in order to save money, the original theatre was not taken down when the permanent building went up. The latter was simply erected over and around the tent, with superb acoustical results!

Practicing two principles of projection, wide opening and firm closing of your mouth as you speak, and adjusting your speech energy to the acoustics of the hall you speak in will do much to help you immediately to powerful speech. Put both into effect as you undertake the series of projection exercises which follow. Since as an actor you will want not only to increase the quantity of your speech but also to improve its quality, you should continue directly with the next six chapters of the book. They explain the theory and practice of the speech techniques which will help you work towards achieving your best possible speech for the stage.

Projection Exercises

NOTE: Each of the exercises below is a combined listening and speaking exercise.

DIRECTIONS: Before beginning, do a voice warm-up. See the warm-up series at the end of this book (immediately preceding the index).

1. Stand facing a fellow-actor, a few feet away from him. If possible, work on a large stage or in a hall or classroom 30 or 40 feet long. Choose a poem that you and he both know by

heart. A Shakespearean sonnet is always a good choice. Say the first two lines yourself, trying to open your mouth well. Go slowly, and listen to the sounds you make. Have your fellow-actor reply to you with the second couplet, with matching speech action. Both of you now take several long steps backward from each other. Then alternately speak the next two couplets with vigorous mouth openings, making each voice sound as loud to the other person as when you were nearer. Repeat the backward walk, and continue to speak couplets to one another over this new distance, maintaining the same openness with added force as necessary. Finally, retreat from each other to the extremities of the room or stage. Now speak one line each of the final couplet with wide mouth openings and firm closings. Try to make your speech carry with the same loudness as the first exchange did.

2. Set up a tape recorder with its microphone 10 feet away from you. If possible, use a microphone like Electro Voice Model 630, which will have enough power to pick up your voice at that distance or more. Record yourself speaking a poem or a prose paragraph. Open your lips well as you do so. Play back the recording, and note how successfully you projected your speech. Increase the distance of the microphone from you with successive repetitions, trying to match your first recording in volume. Continue until you reach the limits of the microphone's pick-up power.

3. Do this exercise with a group of fellow-actors in the largest theatre auditorium available to you. Place half the group on the stage, the other half in the back row of the top balcony. Use a poem or speech that all know by heart. An actor on the stage begins by speaking out the first line or sentence, throwing it to his opposite number in the balcony, who will reply with the second line. Actor Number 3 on the stage will continue with the third line, answered by Actor Number 4 in the balcony. Continue in this way until all have spoken.

Easy naturalness of mouth and breath action resulting in full projection should be the objective. Any shouting or forcing of lines will be discouraged by the continuous nature of the exercise and by the example of those who project their speech easily and fully without strain.

4. This exercise has three parts:
    a. Speak the following poem with "Oh" ringing out more and more strongly through the piece.
    b. Dividing the group as in exercise 3, take alternate groups of lines, calling them to each other.
    c. Speak the poem as a group chant, growing in exultation throughout, until the last five lines when the mood changes to supplication.

MY LORD, WHAT A MORNING

Oh, my Lord,
What a morning.

Oh, my Lord,
What a feeling,
When Jack Johnson
Turned Jim Jeffries'
Snow-white face
Up to the ceiling.

Yes, my Lord,
Fighting is wrong.
But what an uppercut!

Oh, my Lord,
What a morning.

Oh, my Lord,
What a feeling,
When Jack Johnson
Turned Jim Jeffries'
Lily-white face
Up to the ceiling.

Oh, my Lord,
What a morning.

Oh, my Lord,
Take care of Jack.
Keep him, Lord,
As you made him,
Big, and strong, and black.

WARING CUNEY

5. End each series of exercises in this book by applying projection to the material you have just worked on. (More exercises for projection appear in Appendix C.)

4 | ~

The Speech Instrument

I have never known a more engaging creature.
...He loved...to exercise his lungs and
muscles, and to speak and laugh with his
whole body.
ROBERT LOUIS STEVENSON, *In the South Seas*

A STRONG, clear, flexible, and compelling voice is both an
asset in itself and a necessity for acting or for projected
speech of any kind. Such speech has special attributes
which set it apart from the speech of the man in the
street—depth and fullness of resonance, brilliance of articulation, impeccable pronunciation, infinite flexibility, and
tireless power. Given these, the speaker who uses them
with taste can make an art of communication by the
spoken word.

The instrument which produces this speech is the group
of interconnected bodily organs shown in Figure 1, called
the *vocal tract*. The primary functions of these organs are
breathing and eating. Unlike these, speech is an overlaid
function, learned, not instinctive. It is learned by ear in
childhood, in much the same way that one learns to play
the piano by ear. But to become a good musician, one
must study one's instrument and consciously improve all
the skills of the art. It is the same with speech. It is helpful
to begin by learning how the parts of the vocal tract work
together to make the sounds of speech.

The vocal tract may be thought of as a machine that
produces sound. It consists first of a power mechanism,

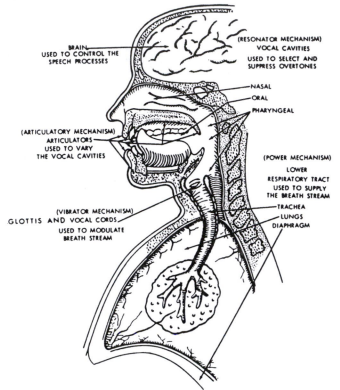

FIGURE 1. The Vocal Tract.

the lower respiratory tract. This includes the *diaphragm,
lungs,* and *trachea* (Figure 1). At the top of the trachea
is a vibrator mechanism, the vocal cords within the larynx.
Above is a resonating and articulating mechanism—the
throat, mouth, and nose, labeled in the drawing as the
vocal cavities, pharyngeal, oral, and nasal. Finally, there
is a feedback and control system, the ear, brain, and con-
necting nervous system. These systems function simultaneously to generate a moving column of air, to vibrate it
in the larynx for voiced sounds, to constrict or stop it in
the mouth for unvoiced sounds, and, by a continuing
combination of the three, to produce speech.

The act of speech is so familiar that you may not be at all aware of its interrelated processes. Most of the organs involved are hidden from sight within the body. Yet as they move in speech, many of their movements are apparent on the outside of the body. Watch your own abdomen, chest, neck, and face in a mirror as you breathe and speak, and you will learn much about the patterns of movement that occur during speech. Place your fingertips on the parts of the body that move, and sense the direction and depth of the movements. You should also listen to your own speech, noting any change in its quality as you alter any movement. Finally, by studying the diagrams in this chapter, you may relate the facts they present to what you see, feel, and hear as you speak. This should give you a clear picture of what is happening and a good understanding of how you may control it for best results.

In addition to the action which produces speech, you must understand the nature of the product. As was discussed in Chapter 3, speech is made up of pressure pulses. The pulses consist of alternate rarefactions and condensations of the air. These disturbances travel out in all directions from the source of the disturbance, which in speech is the vibratory mechanism, the vocal cords. The air itself does not travel when a sound is made. The pressure pulses travel through it somewhat as wind ripples travel over a field of wheat. But the pulses of sound get fainter as they travel further, finally dying out altogether. The stronger the vibrations at the source, the more powerful will be the pressure pulses and the farther they will travel.

When a listener is in the path of the pressure pulses, his outer ear collects them, and they pass down the ear canal to his eardrum. They strike the drum, making it vibrate with the exact patterns of which they are composed. The vibrations are transformed in the inner ear to nerve impulses. These travel up the nerve of hearing to the brain. The brain receives these impulses as signals which it recognizes as speech sounds.

The process is the same whether the sound waves originate from another speaker or from your own mouth. With practice, you can concentrate on listening to the sound of your own voice. If your own speech as you hear it does not satisfy you, your brain may direct the various organs of the vocal tract to modify their actions until the speech result pleases you. This in essence is how the ear acts as a feedback system to control speech for the stage.

The moving column of air which is required for speech is provided by breath exhaled from the lungs. It must first be inhaled, drawn in by the breathing muscles which are the power mechanism of the system. The main one is the *diaphragm*, a big dome-shaped sheet of muscle lying under the chest cavity (Figure 1). It acts as an air pump, flattening itself downward on its work stroke, then relaxing upward. The diaphragm as it flattens downward widens and deepens the space inside the chest (Figure 2*a*). At the same time the ribs at the sides swing up and out sideways, pulled by the intercoastal muscles. They act like a bellows, helping to widen the chest cavity. Within this cavity are

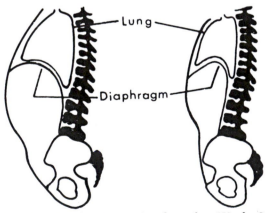

FIGURE 2. The Diaphragm (*a*) after the Work Stroke, (*b*) Relaxed.

the *lungs,* two elastic spongy organs whose air spaces all connect. They lead to tubes called the *bronchi* and thence to the windpipe, or trachea (Figures 1 and 3). When the chest in which they are confined enlarges as the diaphragm flattens, air rushes in through the nose or mouth or both, down the trachea and into the lungs. This is *inhalation.*

Do not allow anyone to tell you that you need to learn to breathe with the diaphragm for speech. You know how to do this already and have always known it, for there is no other way. When you were born, your diaphragm made a great plunge, drawing air into your lungs for the first time. Immediately you let this air out in a cry, your first utterance, and at once your diaphragm plunged again to pump in more air for your second cry. Since then it has been pumping away, pulling in air for every breath you take and for every word you speak. The act is controllable because the diaphragm, which normally works independently as the heart does, may be taken over and made to pump harder or faster by the conscious brain. This conscious control is important because strong, swift inhalations are needed for powerful speech.

Exhalation reverses the process of inhalation. The dia-

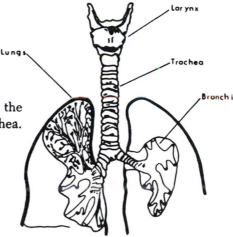

FIGURE 3. The Lungs, the Bronchi, and the Trachea.

phragm relaxes up to its dome shape, and the ribs sink back at the sides (Figure 2b). As the stretched chest cavity shrinks back to its normal size, its elastic recoil exerts pressure on the lungs. They are squeezed from below upward and from the sides inward as one squeezes a tube of toothpaste. Out comes a current of air up the trachea and through the nose and mouth. This happens at each exhalation.

Breathing of this kind goes on when you are silent. When you speak, you speed up the inhalation and slow down the exhalation. You use the upgoing current of air as the source of your sound energy. As a current of water is made to drive a turbine by being forced through a narrow channel, so the air current is made to drive the vibrator mechanism by being forced through a much-narrowed opening between the vocal cords or folds. This space is called the *glottis*, shown in Figures 1 and 5 at the top of the trachea. It is a triangular-shaped opening, formed by the vocal cords which lie across the trachea in the larynx. The larynx, a ringlike structure, is the modified top section of the trachea. You can feel its front part moving up and down when you swallow. The ring of the larynx surrounds and protects the vocal cords, which are like folds or lips lying across it. The space between them, normally open, is closed for phonation by the two pivoting arytenoid cartilages (Figure 4). Like closed lips, they block the upcoming air current until you make it strong enough to force them to open a little for a fraction of a second. Because they are under tension, the cords do not stay open but open and close with a fluttering motion, like lips whirring, as long as the pressure on them continues. Their vibrations start the air above them vibrating as sound waves, which travel on through the mouth into the surrounding air. The energy of air pressure has now been turned into the energy of sound.

This sound is not yet speech. Its waves will be trans-

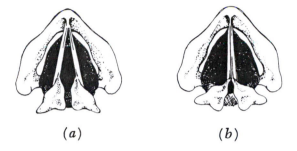

(a)   (b)

FIGURE 4. The Larynx, seen from above. The vocal folds are opened for breathing (*a*), closed for phonation (*b*).

formed into the sound waves of speech by resonance and articulation. This happens in the hollow spaces above the larynx formed by the throat, mouth, and nose and called the *vocal cavities* (Figure 1). Excluding the nose, these form a continuous, roughly horn-shaped space about 7 inches long (Figures 1 and 5). The tip of the horn is back down at the *larynx;* the open end is forward at the lips. This is not a rigid horn, however. Its spaces can be altered in size and shape. Its rear part, the *pharynx,* is lined with muscular tissue and can raise or lower the larynx below it. Its front part is the mouth, a chamber of changeable size by virtue of its elastic cheeks, movable soft palate, hinged jaw, mobile lips, and, above all, a tongue that can move its tip, middle, and back independently up and down against the inner boundaries of the mouth. The action of the tongue is therefore of the greatest importance in producing clear speech.

The nose is an additional air space. It is coupled into the system by the action of the soft palate (Figure 6). When you breathe through the nose with lips closed, the *uvula,* which is the tip of the soft palate, is held away from the wall of the pharynx and the air passage through the nose is open. When the uvula is held up and back against

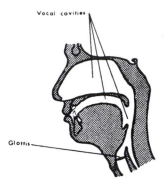

FIGURE 5. Cross Section of the Head. The continuity of the passages for speech waves from the glottis into the throat, mouth, and nose can be clearly seen.

the wall of the pharynx, it shuts off the nasal cavity from the passage of speech vibrations. This is its normal position during speech. It should open only to sound m, n, or ng.

In speech, all the parts of the vocal mechanism function together, sending out continuous chains of sound. As an actor, you need to understand both the process in general, as described in this chapter, and the detailed special functions of each part. The exercises below are simple means of permitting you to observe externally the various parts of your own vocal tract in action. You also need to learn to make each part function so as to produce powerful speech easily.

The chapters which follow are arranged in order of the action of the vocal organs. They include exercises which will guide you in training their action. Chapter 5 explains the necessity of relaxation during speech. Chapter 6 deals with the breathing mechanism and its importance in speech production. It includes exercises that will help you to learn to breathe so as to produce the stronger, clearer speech, which is a necessity for the actor.

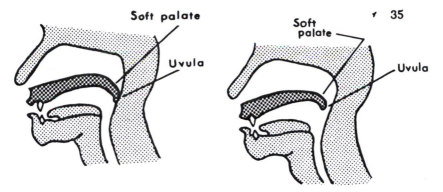

FIGURE 6. Action of the Uvula. Left, resting against the palate for all sounds except *m, n,* and *ng.* Right, lowered for *m, n,* and *ng.*

Exercises for Observation of the
Speech Mechanism in Action

1. *Observation of Inhalation and Exhalation*
   a. Directly after vigorous exercise, such as modern dance practice, while you are still breathing quickly and deeply, watch the action of your thorax and abdomen. When your rate of breathing slows down, observe that the degree of expansion of the thorax and abdomen is directly related to the strength and depth of the inhalation.
   b. Counting aloud slowly and loudly, inhaling after every five counts, observe the expansion of the thorax and abdomen as before.

2. *Observation of the Vibrations of Speech.* Wrists touching, cup your hands under your chin and around your face, fingers firmly on your cheeks and nostrils. Recite aloud your name, the date, and your address, over and over. Feel the vibrations in the pharynx, cheeks, and nose as you do so.

Keeping your fingers still in position, lip the same words. Next, whisper them. Finally, speak them very softly. Observe at what point vibrations begin again in each part.

3. *Observation of Articulation during Speech.* Observe on television any news broadcaster with whom you are familiar. As he reaches his signing-off sequence, turn off the sound and watch his articulation. Can you understand what he says?

4. *Watching Your Own Movements in Speech.* Speak the poem below, watching in a mirror your lip and jaw movements and your expansion during breathing. Speak vigorously and fast.

THE SONG OF THE UNGIRT RUNNERS

We swing ungirded hips
And lighten'd are our eyes,
The rain is on our lips,
We do not run for prize.
We know not whom we trust,
Nor whitherward we fare,
But we run because we must
   Through the great wide air.

The waters of the seas
Are troubled as by storm.
The tempest strips the trees
And does not leave them warm.
Does the tearing tempest pause?
Do the tree-tops ask it why?
So we run without a cause
   'Neath the big bare sky.

The rain is on our lips,
We do not run for prize.
But the storm the water whips
And the wave howls to the skies.
The winds arise and strike it
And scatter it like sand,
And we run because we like it
   Through the broad bright land.

CHARLES HAMILTON SORLEY

5 | ᴞ

Relaxation for Speech

> If an actor can develop in himself the habit of
> freeing his body from superfluous tensions, he
> removes one of the most substantial blocks to
> creative activity.
> Constantin Stanislavski, *Stanislavski's Legacy*

In the quotation above, Stanislavski declares that, for the
actor, freedom from tension results in freedom for creative
activity. This chapter will show how freedom from tension
in the throat and in the breathing mechanism also releases
the actor's natural voice. Once the obstructions that these
tensions produce have been removed, the speech may flow
out more easily, naturally, beautifully, and strongly. The
removal of tension thus becomes the first step in the
actor's speech training program.

The mark of a good natural voice is its pleasant quality.
The pleasantness of speech is a direct result of the relaxation of the vocal tract. If there is tension in any part of it,
in the breathing muscles, trachea, larynx, throat, or mouth,
there may be a constriction of the passage for speech at
the point where the tension exists. This will block its
natural outflow. It will cause strain in the sound and
fatigue in its production. If, on the other hand, the whole
vocal tract is relaxed, the passageways will be fully open
and all the mechanisms of speech production may function
smoothly and efficiently.

The actor in training must achieve this relaxation under
all conditions. He must learn to keep the vocal tract free

and relaxed no matter what he may be doing on the stage. He may be sitting, standing, walking, or running; he may be cramped into difficult positions if the role requires it; his body may even be tensed as for a spring. But he keeps this tension out of the vocal tract. There, no matter how the body is contracted, relaxation is the rule. It is a central core of ease and openness. Tensions may come and go as the actor wills in the various muscle groups of the body, even in those which lie near the vocal tract, without affecting its relaxed state in the least.

The actor achieves this habitual condition on the stage from long practice of a simple series of exercises. These result in relaxation of the whole body and of the vocal tract alone. You need both because you may have residual tensions of which you are almost unaware. If, for example, the carriage of your body is not perfect, tensions of the back or neck muscles may be pulling it out of line. If you often frown, tension may be latent in the muscles of your forehead. This could be a problem because any bodily tensions tend to spread from one muscle group to another nearby. Tensions in the face, neck, and shoulders in particular affect the vocal tract adversely, so you must begin with the relaxation of the upper trunk. To achieve this as quickly as possible, do the relaxation exercises lying on your back on the floor, as described in the exercise section of this chapter. You will learn to relax the muscles of the body group by group, including the chest and neck muscles, finishing with those of the upper vocal tract. The exercise series ends with a yawn which opens the throat and mouth wide, then subsides, leaving the jaw, lips, tongue, and pharynx relaxed. Eventually you will be able to relax the vocal tract simply by doing those relaxation exercises which relate to the shoulders, neck, and head, but for some time you should undertake the whole series. The deep relaxation which results will benefit the entire body as well as the speaking voice.

The benefit to speech is both acoustical and mechanical. Acoustically, the wide mouth and the open throat make better resonators than they do when they are constricted by tension as will be fully explained in the chapter dealing with resonance in speech tone. Mechanically, the muscles of the tongue, soft palate, lips, and jaw must move rapidly and with great precision for long periods during the act of speech. They function most smoothly and accurately when they are relaxed to begin with.

As an actor undertaking speech training, therefore, you must master the entire series of relaxation exercises. Thereafter, you must practice them regularly. Your practice periods for this part of your exercise program may be brief. Five to ten minutes is usually enough to achieve a feeling of relaxation which you will soon recognize and enjoy. As soon as you have reached it, you may proceed to the other exercises.

Be careful, however, not to omit this first group. Relaxation underlying your speech for the stage will be important to you all your professional life. It will enable you to handle long and difficult roles night after night without loss of voice. Lack of this relaxation in the untrained speaker makes him become hoarse during a series of campaign speeches or a lecture tour. Strain causes bodily fatigue and tension which soon spreads to the vocal tract. Huskiness begins, and laryngitis and complete loss of voice may follow. During your training years, you, too, may experience great fatigue during public performances. As a student, you must attend your classes by day and then rehearse or perform at night. Only the repeated practice of relaxation, both through the day and shortly before each performance, will safeguard you from the possible onset of hoarseness. Because the exercises have a calming effect, they also tend to free you from nervous tension and stage fright. But, most important of all, when relaxation always accompanies the speech act, it steadily promotes the production of smooth, resonant tone. Eventually, however vigorous the movement of your body on the stage, however violent your gestures and intense your facial expression, a condition of relaxation will prevail in the vocal tract. This will enable your speech to continue with minimum effort and maximum tone.

Relaxation Exercises

GENERAL DIRECTIONS: Groups A, B, and C below call for muscle contractions and releases. The contractions should be sharp and brief, lasting only a moment. The releases should last for at least 30 seconds each, the body being perfectly still until a new contraction is made. Each of the first three groups closes with an energizing of the body to carry it from the limpness of relaxation into poised readiness for action.

GROUP A. LYING-DOWN RELAXATION EXERCISES

To Begin: Lie on the floor on your back, arms at your sides. Wear loose clothing. Unfasten your belt or waist band.

1. *Arms.* Stretch your right arm straight up in the air, rigid, fist clenched. Hold this position momentarily. Then drop the arm heavily to the floor. Let it lie there loose and limp. Repeat the exercise with the other arm. Rest for 30 seconds or more.

2. *Legs.* Stretch both legs straight out and clench the feet, bending the toes sharply down so that the feet are arched. Hold very briefly. Let go, so that the legs and feet lie limp like the arms. Rest for 30 seconds or more.

3. *Buttocks.* Contract the buttocks as tightly as possible. Relax them. Rest.

4. *Spine.* Flatten the spine to the floor. Relax it. Rest.

5. *Shoulders.* Round the shoulders forward sharply, so that they are lifted from the floor. Drop them back again. Rest.

6. *Neck.* Turn the head to the right without lifting it from the floor. Feel the left side of the neck stretched, the right side pulling. Release the head back to a relaxed position, the eyes looking up. Repeat to the left. Release it back, and rest. Draw the chin down on the chest so that the head is lifted from the floor. Release it back again. Rest.

7. *Face*
   a. Close the eyes tightly. Relax them, letting them open. Rest.
   b. Open the eyes as wide as possible, wrinkling the brow. Relax them to a half-open position. Rest.
   c. Frown, drawing the eyebrows together hard. Release the frown. Rest.
   d. With lips closed, smile as widely as possible. Stop smiling. Rest.
   e. Open the mouth as widely as possible. Inhale deeply. Sigh and slowly yawn out the air.
   f. Repeat, yawning more deeply and vocalizing gently on the prolonged yawn, *Aaaaah!*

8. *Rest Period.* Lie quietly, feeling the pleasant limpness of all the muscle groups. Allow them to become more and more deeply relaxed. Remain at rest for several minutes. Observe the quiet rise and fall of the abdomen at the waist as the breath passes in and out of the lungs.

9. *Getting Up from Relaxation.* Get up very gradually, as described below, avoiding any sharp, quick movements.
   a. From the lying position, pull with the right shoulder and hip, rolling over on to your left side. Pull your knees gently up to your chin, curling your head down to meet them. Keep your head on the floor.
   b. Place your right hand on the floor, palm down. Push with the right hand and left elbow until you are on

your knees. Draw one knee up under you, until the foot is on the floor. Repeat with the other knee, and slowly raise the hips until the legs are straight, feet apart. Leave the trunk, head, and arms hanging loosely down from the waist. Steady the body in this position. Be sure the head hangs down, the neck being fully relaxed.

c. Slowly draw the trunk upward, pulling with the muscles of the lower back, straightening the spine joint by joint, feeling each vertebra coming to rest on the one below it. Unroll the spine into the erect position, head and arms still hanging heavy and loose.

d. Raise the head slowly, like a weight which you set on the top of the spinal column, the arms meanwhile falling into their natural positions at the sides of the body. The whole body should now feel straight and tall, well supported, relaxed, and free.

10. *Energization.* Energize the body, springing a little on the feet, swinging the arms lightly, moving the head easily. Feel the balance of this posture. The body is erect, the head comfortably poised on top. This is the basic posture for all speech practice.

GROUP B. SITTING-DOWN RELAXATION EXERCISES

To begin: Sit with your back against the back of a straight chair, hands in your lap.

1. *Arms.* Stretch them out in front one by one. Relax as in the first group, dropping hands into your lap. Rest.

2. *Legs.* Stretch them out stiffly, toes pointed down, feet clenched as in Group A, 2, above. Relax, letting the feet rest on the floor.

3. *Buttocks.* Clench them so that the body is lifted a little from the seat of the chair. Relax them. Rest.

4. *Shoulders.* Drop arms to your sides. Round the shoulders, turning the hands inward. Relax, returning hands to your lap. Rest.

5. *Neck.* Hang the head. In this position, turn it to right and left as in Group A, 6. Rest.

6. *Face.* With head still hanging, do the facial exercises described in Group A, 7. Finish with deep inhalations and yawns, allowing the head to swing upwards as the air is exhaled.

7. *Energization.* Energize the body into an upright, supported, sitting position.

GROUP C. STANDING SERIES

To begin: Stand erect with feet apart. Wear low-heeled shoes or none.

1. *Arms.* As in the lying-down series, stretch out each arm to the front in turn, fists clenched. Drop each heavily to the side. Rest.

2. *Feet.* Clench the feet, arching them as much as possible. Release them. Rest.

3. *Knees.* Lock the knees back sharply. Release them. Rest.

4. *Buttocks.* Clench the buttocks. Release them. Rest.

5. *Shoulders.* Round the shoulders, keeping the arms loose. Release them. Rest.

6. *Neck.* Hang the head. Turn it to the right and the left as in Group A, 6. Rest.

7. *Face.* With hanging head, do the facial exercises as described in Group A, 7. Yawn and sigh as in Group B, 6. Rest.

8. *Energization.* Energize the body as in Group A, 10.

GROUP D. TRANSITION EXERCISES

Use the following exercises to prepare for the active work of speech and to induce deep relaxation in the shoulders and neck, where residual tensions may linger.

To begin: Stand with the feet apart for greater stability.

1. *Bobbing.* Stand with feet apart. Hang the trunk and arms down heavily from the waist, stretching loosely down with the fingers, touching the floor if you can. Bob down and halfway up several times. Finally uncurl slowly into the erect position. Repeat, increasing your speed, bobbing easily up and down.

2. *Swaying.* Stand with trunk, head, and arms hanging from the waist. Sway the trunk and arms freely and rhythmically from side to side. Finally, raise the trunk to the erect position.

3. *Circling.* Stand with trunk and arms hanging. Begin by swaying from side to side as before. Build the swaying up to a vigorous swing that carries trunk and arms well out to each side. Complete with a very strong swing, carrying the trunk and arms up, over, and around in a full circle. On the rebound, continue two or three more strong swings, the last of which pushes the trunk and arms up and over into a sweeping circle in the opposite direction. This exercise stretches and strengthens all the muscles around the waist, loosens the shoulder and neck muscles, and brings a general feeling of vigor and freedom into the upper trunk. It is an excellent preparation for strong speech.

4. *Arm Swinging*
   a. Stand erect, arms loosely at the sides.

b. Count 1, 2, 3 in waltz time, swinging the arms as follows, with the count.
   - (1) Lift arms, swing arms forward and up to shoulder level, shoulder width apart.
   - (2) Bounce arms, swinging them down, then out and up on the rebound, sideways to shoulder level.
   - (3) Circle arms, swinging them down again, forward, and up over the head, bringing them down to the sides, ready for the count of 1 again. The exercise is continuous.

5. *Head Rolling.* This exercise is sometimes called the "Cannon Ball" because it treats the head as if it were a heavy ball rolling in a socket. Hold the body tall and easily erect, feet apart. Hang the head down heavily, chin on chest. Slowly circle the head around, letting it fall on one shoulder, then back, with the chin pointing upward, over on the other shoulder, and so back into place. Do it lazily, eyes and mouth half-open. Repeat in the reverse direction. The key words for this exercise are SLOW, SMOOTH, and CONTINUOUS. When you get the feel of it, begin to inhale on the first half of each circle and exhale on the second half. If you yawn while doing it, so much the better. If you do not yawn, try the following exercise.

6. *Prolonged Yawning.* Drop the head forward as before. Slowly swing it straight up and back, opening the mouth wide and drawing in breath through the mouth and nose. Droop it slowly forward again, breathing out all the air through the mouth. This usually induces a natural yawn. Enjoy it, let it stretch the back of the throat and the glottis fully. It does for the pharynx and larynx what a good stretch does for a tired back and shoulders.

GROUP E. SPEAKING WITH DEEPLY RELAXED TONE

1. The following poem, "Zimbabwe" (Zim-*bahb*-way), was written by a black Rhodesian about the famous ancient ruin

from which the country now takes its name. Sitting, standing, or lying down, deeply relaxed, speak the poem with slow, quiet speech, still fully audible. Give full value to the many bell-like "l" sounds in the poem. Try to catch its trance-like mood. Find others to read the same way.

ZIMBABWE
(After the Ruins)

I want to worship stone
Because it is Silence
I want to worship Rock
so, hallowed be its silence

for in the beginning there was
  silence
and we all were
and in the end there will be
  silence
and in the end we all will be.

Silence speaks to fool and
  wise-man
to slave and king
to deaf and dumb
to blind-man
and to thunder even

for in the beginning there was
  silence
and we all were
and in the end there will be
  silence
and in the end we all will be.

The mind that dreamt this
  dream
massively reaching unto time
  and space
the voice that commanded
the talent that wove the
  architecture . . .

All speak Silence now—Silence.

And behold these stones,
the visible end of silence,
and when I lie in my grave
when the epitaph is forgotten
Stone and Bone will speak,
reach out to you in no sound,
so mysteries will weave in your
  mind
when I'm gone

Because silence cradles all—
the space and the universe—
and touches all.

M. B. Zimunya

2. More exercises for relaxed readings appear in Appendix C.

6 | ⤳

Breath Control for Speech

This air, which by life's law
My lung must draw and draw
Now but to breathe its praise.
GERARD MANLEY HOPKINS

THE SECOND STEP you must take towards freeing the natural voice is to achieve proper breath control for speech. As with relaxation, so with breathing during speech: ease promotes excellence. The breath that you use to speak with is exhaled naturally as part of the act of breathing for life. The air that was taken in to provide the body with oxygen must go out again, carrying waste gases with it. It passes out as a moving air current, available for the making of speech sounds. In speech, as was explained in Chapter 3, inhalations are naturally quicker and exhalations are slower than in quiet breathing. In speech for the stage, this change becomes more marked. Inhalation is fast and full. Exhalation is slow and smooth, but strong. The air is released easily and naturally in a steady, ample current that produces clear, carrying speech tone. Unobstructed, it pours up as from a fountain.

That there may always be a full flow of air upward, inhalations in stage speech must be timed to refill the lungs as soon as you feel the air pressure in them getting low. This feeling, that you are "running out of breath," is the signal for you to pause for a fraction of a second as soon as the sense of the line you are speaking allows it and pump in a large volume of air with a vigorous downward stroke of your diaphragm. Your body profile will change, expanding at the waist and sides as shown in Plate III. Immediately thereafter your diaphragm will begin to relax upwards, slowly resuming its domed shape. Your ribs will sink at the sides, and your chest cage will contract by elastic recoil. No more than this normal muscular action is required to provide the needed current of air. You will turn this easily into speech as long as it lasts and then inhale quickly at the next possible pause. An essential skill for you, as for a singer, is timing this fast, full intake of air for the moment of need.

This natural exhalation of air for stage speech is effected by release of the muscles contracted during inhalation. Usually no conscious effort need accompany the release. Control needs to be applied to inhalation only. Under certain circumstances, however, control must be applied to exhalation also. These circumstances are those in which you must pour out a flood of passionate speech for a longer period of time than usual without pausing to refill your lungs. Probably the action on the stage is rising to a climax; rage or fear or hope or joy is in full flood. To continue unchecked speech, using the flow of air from your lungs as long as possible, you must go on from natural released exhalation to controlled exhalation. From releasing the diaphragm muscle, you proceed to the contracting of its antagonist muscles, those of the abdominal wall. You slowly draw in your waist, contracting the front of the abdomen. This presses its contents upwards against the diaphragm, which in turn is pressed up against the lungs. You will effect a change in body profile such as is shown in Plate III. Pulling in your waist as much as possible, you will empty the lungs far more fully than usual. You will be able to speak in full voice much longer than you normally do before you inhale again. In contrast to the natural exhalation accomplished by release, this controlled exhalation is accomplished by contraction.

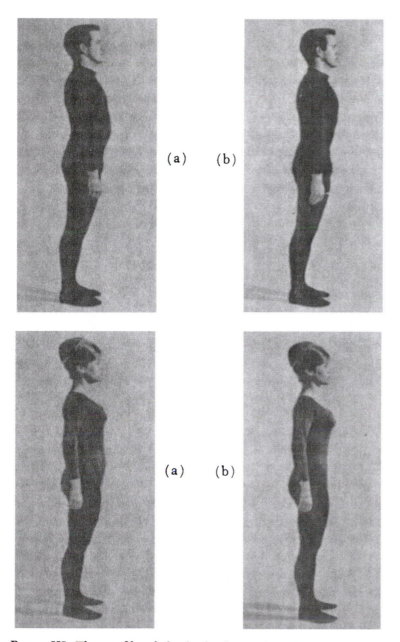

Plate III. The profile of the body during breathing: (a) after inhalation; (b) after exhalation

Great actors use this technique for powerful passages like the climax of the famous speech beginning, "Once more into the breach, dear friends," in Shakespeare's *Henry V*. Olivier, in a recording no longer listed,° read these lines with one breath taken at the beginning, and only one more taken after the word "start." Thereafter, the intensity, pitch, and speed of the delivery all rose together to a tremendous climax, a long cry on the word "George!" for which there was still plenty of breath available.

> There is none of you so mean and base,
> That hath not noble lustre in your eyes.
> I see you stand like greyhounds in the slips,
> Straining upon the start. The game's afoot;
> Follow your spirit, and upon this charge
> Cry "God for Harry, England, and Saint George!"

The spacing of your inhalations for stage speech, whether between released or contracted exhalations, will develop as you work the selection up to performance level. The same process may be applied during a sequence of rehearsals. As you bring your lines to the speed of performance, the spaces between inhalations will tend to lengthen. The spacing will finally settle into a workable pattern of intake of air at certain places in the script and outflow of air in speech between them. After this it will vary little from rehearsal to rehearsal. The pattern must insure that the air current during any exhalation is strong enough from beginning to end to deliver the last syllables as firmly as the first. This will enable you to avoid a fault commonly attributed to the American actor, the failure to project the last word or syllable of a sentence or phrase. This fault makes it hard for the audience to follow the dialogue and so hinders comprehension and enjoyment of the play. Yet it is as needless as it is maddening. Proper spacing of inhalations readily corrects it.

In addition to contraction for controlled exhalation as

° RCA Victor, LM 1924.

described above, contractions of a special kind are needed for an exclamation such as a cry or a shriek on the stage. A shriek is always uttered suddenly and with great force. To produce it, a blast of air must be sent up the trachea against the vocal cords. In order to accomplish this, you must first plan the exact moment in which to fill the lungs extra full, to provide force for the shriek. If it occurs in the middle of one of your lines, choose a moment just preceding, where a fraction of a second's pause will give you a chance to snatch the deep, full breath required. If the scream follows another actor's line, you must inhale just as he is finishing that line. Breathe in hard during his last three syllables. Then, as your cue comes, at the instant of uttering "Oh!," "Aaaaah!," "Help!," or whatever the cry may be, set your mouth in the shape of the word, pull in hard and suddenly at the waist, and drive out the sound as a cry. The force of the contraction will send the air up the trachea and through the vocal cords suddenly and sharply. The word or words of the cry will be ejected like a dart from a blowgun. The sound waves will explode away from the glottis in a violent pressure disturbance. This is forced exhalation. All the force used comes from a single sharp contraction of the muscles of the abdominal wall. No force at all is used in the throat. This makes it possible for you to scream without strain and without any danger to the larynx. At the same time, it enables you to reach a climax of intense emotion. Such a climax was reached by John Barrymore in Hamlet's speech, "Ah, what a rogue and peasant slave am I!" In his recording, the speech begins at low pitch and low intensity. It mounts and mounts, suddenly surging up on the line,

Remorseless, treacherous, lecherous, kindless villain!

rising to a final, violent shriek:

Aaaah, vengeance!

Its effect in actual performance must have been electric.

Laughter in a role also requires a special kind of control of exhalation. You break into a laugh on the stage partly by emotional, partly by physical means. You may recall an amusing experience to help you experience humorous feelings vicariously. Without further stimulus, you may begin to laugh as your sense of the comic takes over. But since this process cannot be counted on every time, the act of reproducing physically the muscular contractions of laughter, as explained in the following exercises, can trigger a natural laugh. The two can work together.

Once you have begun laughing, it is easy to continue, for the action and the emotion mutually stimulate each other. The contractions which are both the cause and the effect of laughter are identical with those of panting. The diaphragm contracts lightly, quickly, rhythmically, sending out puffs of breath which have the familiar "huh-huh" sound. These puffs are nearly voiceless, and a great many can be produced between one inhalation and the next. They sound almost exactly like laughter. Rhythmical panting, followed by bursts of vocalizing panting, will merge easily into natural laughter. Real bursts of laughter are spaced by big, noisy inhalations. Often these are vocalized too. You may inhale in this way yourself as your laughter becomes uproarious. Making sounds on indrawn breath is strenuous, however, and should be tried out cautiously for fear of straining the throat.

Sobbing is physically merely a variant of laughing. Sobs are spasmodic, vocalized, panting ejections of air. You may break into crying in a role by recalling grief, simultaneously uttering sobbing pants. As a psychological effect of this action, you might actually begin to weep.

The exercises on breath control which follow lead up to special exercises for screaming, laughing, and sobbing. Practice these exercises daily until you have mastered them. Use the appropriate kind of breath control in any acting you undertake thereafter. It is true that under the pressure of rehearsal you may not perform the new techniques perfectly. But even if you only approximate them, the quality of your tone and the timing of your inhalations should improve. Continue these as you study Chapter 7, which describes how the voice may be enriched with resonance. Relaxation, breath control, and resonance together will build your tone until it is a rich component of your speech for the stage.

Breath Control Exercises
GROUP A. LISTENING FOR BREATH CONTROL

RECORD: *Homage to Shakespeare* (Argo, mono, NF4; stereo, ZNF4)

1. On side 1, listen to the voices of Laurence Olivier, Michael Redgrave, and Paul Scofield. Listen particularly to the sound of intaken breath which can be faintly heard at intervals. Using a Shakespeare text, mark these places. Judge if the breath was ever taken silently between the places you have marked. Attempt yourself to read the same speeches at the same speed, breathing only at the places marked.

2. One side 1, listen to the voices of Irene Worth and Edith Evans and mark in your text the places where you hear breath taken, as in Exercise 1. One actress inhales more audibly and more frequently than the other. Note how this relates to the emotional content and climactic nature of the speech she reads.

3. Carry out similar exercises with the recorded voices of five actors or actresses of your choice. Rate them in order as to the degree of breath control that they possess.

GROUP B. NORMAL INHALATION WITH
GRADUAL EXHALATION

DIRECTIONS: Exercises 1, 2, 3, and 4 may be undertaken in a standing, sitting, or lying position.

1. Breathe naturally. Observe the waistline rise and sink.

2. Deepen the breathing, inhaling through mouth and nose. Hold the breath a moment. Release it gradually, observing the action at the front and sides of the waist.

3. Breathe in as before. Hold the breath, setting the waist muscles. Round the lips, release the waist muscles slowly, and blow out the air in a silent whistle.

4. Repeat Exercise 3, making the breath last as long as possible without strain.

5. Stand up and walk about during the following. The exercise is continuous.
   a. Walk four long steps, inhaling all the time.
   b. Walk four more steps, holding the breath.
   c. Walk four more steps, exhaling all the time.

6. Stand erect, one arm folded across your waist in front, the other across your back. Inhale, feeling the body expand so that it pushes on both your arms. Slowly exhale.

During all the six exercises above, observe that the natural elastic recoil of the thorax after inhalation is sufficient to send a stream of air upwards for several seconds. No conscious effort is required to maintain it.

GROUP C. INHALATION WITH PANTING EXHALATION

1. Sit in a straight chair, upright but relaxed. Pant rapidly with open mouth but without inhaling, huh-huh-huh! Use a rhythm of seven pants, followed by an inhalation:

Huh-huh-huh-huh-huh-huh-huh: pause, and inhale.
Huh-huh-huh-huh-huh-huh-huh: pause, and inhale.

Observe that with the inhalation, a push downward is felt under the lungs. This is the plunging downstroke of the diaphragm.

2. Pant in a rhythm of three slow *huh's*, followed by a short pause.

> *Huh—huh—huh:* pause, and inhale.
> *Huh—huh—huh:* pause, and inhale.

Again, notice the strong downthrust of the diaphragm at the moment of inhalation. It occurs readily because the panting has nearly emptied the lungs of breath.

3. Pant with strong, single *huh's*, inhaling between each like a dog. Observe how the lungs fill with air at each inhalation, expanding the trunk at and above the waist.

4. Send out the breath in long, slow, panting *huh's*. Inhale with a conscious downthrust of the diaphragm. Take in the air through both mouth and nose.

5. Blow the air out gently through rounded lips until the lungs feel empty. Fill them by pulling the diaphragm down as before.

GROUP D. STRONG INHALATION FOLLOWED BY EXHALATION IN HUMMING AND SPEAKING

1. *Humming*
   a. Hum the air out with lips closed, maintaining a steady *mmmmmmmmmmmmmm!* Use a middle pitch. As you feel the lungs becoming empty, fill them up by drawing in air through mouth and nose by a strong inhalation, using a more vigorous downstroke of the diaphragm than in the previous exercises.
   b. Hum loudly and steadily, moving upward on the eight notes of the scale, starting on a low pitch easy for you. Sustain each pitch on one breath until air pressure in the lungs is reduced so that they need to

be refilled. Then draw in the breath with a vigorous downstroke of the diaphragm, and resume the humming.

c. Hum up the scale as before, but with a series of staccato *m*'s on each pitch: *m-m-m-m-m-m-m-m-m:* pause, and inhale.

2. *Counting*

a. Count aloud slowly, in full voice, sustaining the vowel sounds. Pause between each count to refill with breath. Be sure to pull down the diaphragm deeply for the refill. Count in this way up to 10.

b. Count in a sequence as shown below, pausing after each group to refill strongly.

> *One!* (Refill)
> *One, Two!* (Refill)
> *One, Two, Three!* (Refill)

Continue to 10, inhaling only at the end of each group.

GROUP E. STRONG INHALATION FOLLOWED BY RELEASED EXHALATION IN READING

1. Read the following sentences line by line, using a full voice and inhaling before each:

> I inhale strongly just before I read each line.
> I speak the line easily, without strain.
> I exhale through the mouth as I read aloud.
> I do not now try to control the outflow of breath.
> I give my conscious attention to inhalations only.
> I use the same technique in reading poems like the one below.
> In reading poetry, I inhale either after each line or at the end of two lines.

2. Read the following selection slowly, inhaling at each diagonal. Let the tone flow out powerfully and easily, making the most of each word and phrase.

Vocalism, measure, concentration, determination,
    and the divine power to speak words;/
Are you full-lung'd and limber-lipp'd from long trial?/
    from vigorous practice? from physique?/
Do you move in these broad lands as broad as they?/
Come duly to the divine power to speak words?/
For only at last after many years, after chastity,
    friendship, procreation, prudence, and nakedness,/
After treading ground and breasting river and lake,/
After a loosen'd throat, after absorbing eras, temperaments,
    races,/after knowledge, freedom, crimes,/
After complete faith, after clarifyings, elevations,
    and removing obstructions,/
After these and more, it is just possible there comes
    to a man, a woman, the divine power to speak words;/
Then toward that man or that woman swiftly hasten all—
    none refuse, all attend,/
Armies, ships, antiquities, libraries, paintings,
    machines, cities, hate, despair, amity, pain, theft,
    murder, aspiration, form in close ranks,/
They debouch as they are wanted to march obediently
    through the mouth of that man or that woman./

WALT WHITMAN, *Leaves of Grass*

3. Read the following poem in full voice, inhaling strongly
once or twice during each verse wherever the sense of the line
permits a momentary pause. Do not attempt to continue speaking on the same breath once you have felt failing air pressure
in the lungs.

DO NOT GO GENTLE INTO THAT GOOD NIGHT

Do not go gentle into that good night,
Old age should burn and rave at close of day;
Rage, rage against the dying of the light.

Though wise men at their end know dark is right,
Because their words had forked no lightning they
Do not go gentle into that good night.

Good men, the last wave by, crying how bright
Their frail deeds might have danced in a green bay,
Rage, rage against the dying of the light.

Wild men who caught and sang the sun in flight,
And learn, too late, they grieved it on its way,
Do not go gentle into that good night.

Grave men, near death, who see with blinding sight
Blind eyes could blaze like meteors and be gay,
Rage, rage against the dying of the light.

And you, my father, there on the sad height,
Curse, bless me now with your fierce tears, I pray.
Do not go gentle into that good night
Rage, rage against the dying of the light.

DYLAN THOMAS

4. In the following selections, diagonal bars indicate the places where the reader should take breath. The space from bar to bar is thus a one-breath unit. The bars are spaced further and further apart to provide practice in making one released exhalation serve as long as possible for speech. Read each unit easily in full voice, on one exhalation. If you should feel that your breath may not last you to the next diagonal, speed up your reading, and try to finish the unit without inhaling again. However, you must not strain to finish at any time. Inhale before you actually run out of breath, whether you can finish a unit or not.

MEETING AT NIGHT

The gray sea and the long black land,/
And the yellow half-moon large and low;/
And the startled little waves that leap
In fiery ringlets from their sleep,/
As I gain the cove with pushing prow,
And quench its speed i' the slushy sand./

Then a mile of warm sea-scented beach,
Three fields to cross till a farm appears;
A tap at the pane,/the quick sharp scratch
And blue spurt of a lighted match,
And a voice less loud, thro' its joys and fears,
Than the two hearts beating each to each!/

ROBERT BROWNING

PARTING AT MORNING

Round the cape of a sudden came the sea,
And the sun look'd over the mountain's rim:
And straight was a path of gold for him,
And the need of a world of men for me./

ROBERT BROWNING

THEY ALL WANT TO PLAY HAMLET

They all want to play Hamlet./
They have not exactly seen their fathers killed
Nor their mothers in a frame-up to kill,/
Nor an Ophelia dying with a dust gagging the heart,/
Not exactly the spinning circles of singing golden spiders,/
Not exactly this have they got at nor the meaning of flowers—/
O flowers, flowers slung by a dancing girl—in the saddest play
    the ink fish, Shakespeare, ever wrote;/
Yet they all want to play Hamlet because it is sad like all actors
    are sad,/ and to stand by an open grave with a joker's skull
    in the hand and then to say over slow and say over slow wise,
    keen, beautiful words masking a heart that's breaking,
    breaking,/
This is something that calls and calls to their blood./
They are acting when they talk about it and they know it is
    acting to be particular about it
    and yet: They all want to play Hamlet./

CARL SANDBURG

GROUP F. RELEASED EXHALATION FOLLOWED BY
CONTRACTED EXHALATION

1. The following speech from *Hamlet*, III, iv, is divided by
diagonals into long one-breath units, which require released
exhalation followed by contracted exhalation. The unit of lines
4–10 is especially long. Much practice may be needed before
the seven lines can all be spoken on one breath. They may be
broken into two groups if necessary, or they may be speeded up.
This exercise should be regarded as a means to an end, not an
end in itself. The end is the achievement of a climax of excitement or passion on the stage.

Look here, upon this picture, and on this,
The counterfeit presentment of two brothers./
See what a grace was seated on this brow;/
Hyperion's curls, the front of Jove himself,
An eye like Mars, to threaten and command,
A station like the herald Mercury
New-lighted on a heaven-kissing hill;
A combination and a form indeed.
Where every god did seem to set his seal
To give the world assurance of a man:/
This was your husband./Look you now what follows:
Here is your husband, like a mildew'd ear,
Blasting his wholesome brother./Have you eyes?
Could you on this fair mountain leave to feed,
And batten on this moor?/Ha! have you eyes?/
You cannot call it love, for at your age
The hey-day in the blood is tame, it's humble,
And waits upon the judgement, and what judgement
Would step from this to this?/Sense sure you have,
Else could you not have motion, but sure that sense
Is apoplex'd, for madness would not err,/
Nor sense to ecstasy was ne'er so thrall'd
But it reserv'd some quantity of choice,
To serve in such a difference./ What devil was't
That thus hath cozen'd you at hoodman-blind?
Eyes without feeling, feeling without sight
Ears without hands or eyes, smelling sans all,/
Or but a sickly part of one true sense
Could not so mope./O shame! where is thy blush?/
Rebellious hell,
If thou canst mutine in a matron's bones,
To flaming youth let virtue be as wax
And melt in her own fire:/ proclaim no shame
When the compulsive ardour gives the charge,
Since frost itself as actively doth burn,
And reason panders will./

2. As with Exercise 1, divide the Shakespeare speeches listed below into appropriate breath units, some short, some long. Practice them in full voice. Use released and controlled exhalations as needed.

      a. Henry V, IV, iii. KING HENRY: What's he that wishes so? . . . Saint Crispin's day.

      b. Othello, V, ii. OTHELLO: Behold, I have a weapon, . . . dead, O!

c. *Antony and Cleopatra*, IV, xii. ANTONY: This foul Egyptian . . . Eros, ho!

d. *King Lear*, II, ii. KENT: A knave, a rascal, . . . come your ways.

e. *King John*, III, iv. CONSTANCE: No, I defy all counsel, . . . my sorrow's cure.

GROUP G.   THE SCREAM ON STAGE

The following exercises lead by gradual steps to the scream technique. They should be started gently. More and more force may be added as you discover how to keep your throat relaxed as the scream goes through it. Finally, you will rely altogether on the breath pressure to enforce the scream and avoid any tensing of the throat or larynx.

1. *The Single Scream*

a. Inhale deeply. Contract the abdomen and whisper "Ho."

b. Inhale again. Contract the abdomen and say "Ho!" Feel the energy behind the tone coming from the forced-up air.

c. Inhale deeply and quickly. Then contract the abdomen sharply. At the same instant, say a loud staccato "Ho!"

d. Repeat, but use two successive contractions, crying "Ho, ho!"

e. Repeat, crying "Hoooooooooool," continuing to pull in the abdomen and blow out the sound until the breath is gone.

f. Repeat, pushing out *Ho!, Hi!, Hey!*, each on one breath.

g. Repeat (f) as loudly as you can. Relax and yawn if you feel any strain in the throat.

2. *The Scream within the Speech.* Read the following Shakespeare speeches, inhaling at the diagonals and screaming the italicized word or words. If necessary, snatch a breath in the

middle with which to complete screaming out the rest of the sentence. Share the dialogues with a partner if possible.

HAMLET: Bloody, bawdy villain!/
Remorseless, treacherous, lecherous, kindless villain!/
Ah, vengeance!

(II, iv)

JULIET: O, look,/methinks I see my cousin's ghost
Seeking out Romeo, that did spit his body
Upon a rapier's point./Stay, Tybalt, stay!/
Romeo, I come! this do I drink to thee.

(IV, iii)

HAMLET: You go not 'till I set you up a glass
Where you may see the inmost part of you./
QUEEN: What wilt thou do? Thou wilt not murder me?/
Help, ho!/
POLONIUS (behind): *What ho! help, help, help!/*
HAMLET (drawing): How now, a rat? *Dead, for a ducat, dead!*
POLONIUS (behind): *Oh, I am slain!*
QUEEN: *Oh me what hast thou done?*
HAMLET: Nay, I know not. Is it the king?

(III, iv)

DESDEMONA: O! my fear interprets. What! is he dead?
OTHELLO: Had all his hairs been lives, my great revenge
Had stomach for them all.
DESDEMONA: Alas! he is betray'd and I undone.
OTHELLO: *Out, strumpet!/Weep'st thou for him to my face?/*
DESDEMONA: O! banish me, my lord, but kill me not!/
OTHELLO: *Down, strumpet!/*
DESDEMONA: Kill me tomorrow; let me live tonight!/
OTHELLO: *Nay, if you strive,—/*
DESDEMONA: *But half an hour!/*
OTHELLO: Being done, there is no pause./
DESDEMONA: *But while I say one prayer!/*
OTHELLO: *It is too late.*

(V, ii)

CATESBY: *Rescue, my Lord of Norfolk!/rescue, rescue!/*
The king enacts more wonders than a man,
Daring an opposite to every danger:/
His horse is slain, and all on foot he fights,
Seeking for Richmond in the throat of death./
Rescue, fair lord, or else the day is lost!/

RICHARD: *A horse! a horse!/my kingdom for a horse./*
CATESBY: Withdraw, my lord; I'll help you to a horse./
RICHARD: Slave! I have set my life upon a cast,
    And I will stand the hazard of the die./
    I think there be six Richmonds in the field;/
    Five have I slain today, instead of him.—/
    A horse! a horse! my kingdom for a horse!

                         (V, iv)

3. *The Climactic Scream.* Collect examples of screams that occur at climaxes of dramatic action in plays. Practice the technique within the context of the scene in which the scream occurs. Possible scenes are:

    a. The trial scene in Arthur Miller's *The Crucible.* Mary, breaking down in the face of the other girls' hysteria, outscreams them all.

    b. A silent scream is traditional in Brecht's *Mother Courage.* Mother Courage, in order to preserve herself and her daughter, does not acknowledge that the captured soldier is her son. He is taken off stage and shot. Hearing the drum roll, she must react in utter silence. The actress Helene Weigel (Brecht's wife, who made the part famous), when she appeared in 1949 in the title role in the Deutsches Theatre production, accomplished this by carrying out all the mechanics of a scream except the phonation.

4. *The Climactic Scream Recorded.* Listen to the scream of Hamlet, "*Ah vengeance!*" (II, ii), as recorded by the actors listed below. Rank them in order of theatrical effectiveness, according to your own opinion.

      John Barrymore (Audio Rarities, 2280)
      Laurence Olivier (RCA Victor, LM1924)
      John Gielgud (RCA Victor, LM6007)
      Paul Scofield (Phonodisc, SRS232)
      Richard Burton (Columbia, DOL302)

GROUP H. LAUGHING AND SOBBING ON STAGE

The panting exercises which follow lead gradually to laughing or sobbing. Keep as relaxed as possible while attempting them. The first three are the same as those in Group C but in reverse order.

1. Sitting in a comfortable position, pant rhythmically and slowly, inhaling between each pant.

2. Pant in groups of three, inhaling between each:

Huh-huh-huh: pause, and inhale.

3. Pant seven times quickly and inhale:

Huh-huh-huh-huh-huh-huh-huh: pause, and inhale.

4. Pant in irregular rhythm, vocalizing the pants, letting the pitch rise and fall.

Hah-hah-hah——hah-hah-hah-hah——haaaaaa——
hah-hah

5. Pant in vocalized bursts like laughter. Accent some of the pants by prolonging them. Vary the length of these accents. Vary also the number of the pants which follow each accent. Smile and laugh as soon as you feel the impulse to do so. Follow a succession like that suggested below:

Haaaah! huh-huh-huh-huh, Haaaah! huh-huh-huh,
Haaaah! huh-huh-huh-huh-huh-, etc.

6. Start the laughter with an appropriate comment:

I never heard anything so funny in my life!
huh-huh-huh, huh-huh-huh!

Just to think about it starts me off again!
Haaaah-huh-huh-huh, huh-huh-huh-huh, etc.

7. The following are the closing lines of Somerset Maugham's play *The Circle*. The situation is exceedingly ironic. Unknown to Champion-Cheney, his daughter-in-law, Elizabeth, has just run away with Edward Luton, leaving her husband. Arnold.

Read this scene with two other actors, having previously read the entire play. Build the laughter at the end to a tremendous climax on which the curtain should fall.

Enter Champion-Cheney, rubbing his hands. He is as pleased as Punch.

C.-C.: Well, I think I've settled the hash of that young man.
Lady Kitty: Oh!
C.-C.: You have to get up very early in the morning to get the better of your humble servant.

There is the sound of a car starting.

Lady Kitty: What is that?
C.-C.: It sounds like a car. I expect it's your chauffeur taking one of the maids for a joy-ride.
Porteous: Whose hash are you talking about?
C.-C.: Mr. Edward Luton's, my dear Hughie. I told Arnold exactly what to do and he's done it. What makes a prison? Why, bars and bolts. Remove them, and a prisoner won't want to escape. Clever, I flatter myself.
Porteous: You were always that, Clive, but at the moment you're obscure.
C.-C.: I told Arnold to go to Elizabeth and tell her she could have her freedom. I told him to sacrifice himself all along the line. I know what women are. The moment every obstacle to her marriage with Teddie Luton was removed, half the allurement was gone.
Lady Kitty: Arnold did that?
C.-C.: He followed my instructions to the letter. I've just seen him. She's shaken. I'm willing to bet five hundred pounds to a penny that she won't bolt. A downy old bird, eh? Downy's the word. Downy.

He begins to laugh. They laugh, too. Presently they are all three in fits of laughter. They are still laughing when

THE CURTAIN FALLS

8. Practice laughter as called for in scenes *a* and *b* below.
   a. *Death of a Salesman*, Act II, by Arthur Miller:

   BEN *(chuckling):* So this is Brooklyn, eh?

   Later in the scene:

   WILLY *(laughing):* Oh, nerves of iron, that Biff!

   b. In Brecht's *The Caucasian Chalk Circle*, Act IV, an
   old woman is brought before a judge, accused of
   stealing some cows and a ham. She says a miracle-
   working *Saint Banditus* brought them to her door.
   At this, the Bandit, disguised as a hermit, roars with
   laughter.

9. Listen to recorded examples of laughing and weeping:
   a. Uproarious laughter: Mathilde Casadeus as Nicole,
   in *Le Bourgeois Gentilhomme*, La Comédie Fran-
   çaise, Spoken Arts, 794.
   b. Smothered weeping: John Gielgud as Lear in *Ages of
   Man*, Caedmon, SRS 200 (*Lear*, V, iii):

   Howl, howl, howl, howl! O, you are men of stone!
   Had I your tongues and eyes, I'd use them so
   That heav'n's vault should crack.—She's gone forever—

10. Think about the end of II, i, of Dore Schary's *Sunrise
at Campobello*, where Eleanor Roosevelt *"drops the book, turns
away from the children, and breaks into heartrending sobs."*
Play the scene.

GROUP I. BREATH CONTROL AS A REFLEX ACTION

1. The lines below are from the poem "Lepanto," named
after a great naval battle (1571) in which Ottoman seapower
was destroyed by a Christian crusade. The magnificent poem
is full of clanging sound and dazzling imagery. You should
by now be ready to read it aloud. Forgetting breathing, throw
yourself into its crusading mood and find enough breath
reflexly at the pauses to do the great climax justice.

LEPANTO

White founts falling in the courts of the sun,
And the Soldan of Byzantium is smiling as they run;
There is laughter like the fountains in that face of all men feared,
It stirs the forest darkness, the darkness of his beard,
It curls the blood-red crescent, the crescent of his lips,
For the inmost sea of all the earth is shaken with his ships.
They have dared the white republics up the capes of Italy,
They have dashed the Adriatic round the Lion of the Sea,°
And the Pope has cast his arms abroad for agony and loss,
And called the kings of Christendom for swords about the Cross.
The cold Queen of England is looking in the glass;
The shadow of the Valois°° is yawning at the Mass;
From evening isles fantastical rings faint the Spanish gun,
And the Lord upon the Golden Horn is laughing in the sun.
Dim drums throbbing, in the hills half heard,
Where only on a nameless throne a crownless prince has stirred,
Where, risen from a doubtful seat and half-attainted stall,
The last knight of Europe takes weapons from the wall,
The last and lingering troubadour to whom the bird has sung,
That once went singing southward when all the world was young.

In that enormous silence, tiny and unafraid,
Comes up along a winding road the noise of the Crusade.
Strong gongs groaning as the drums boom far,
Don John of Austria is going to the war,
Stiff flags straining in the night-blasts cold
In the gloom black-purple, in the glint old-gold,
Torchlight crimson on the copper kettle-drums,
Then the tuckets, then the trumpets, then the cannon, and he comes.
Don John laughing in the brave beard curled,
Spurning of his stirrups like the thrones of all the world,
Holding his head up for a flag of all the free.
Love-light of Spain—hurrah!
Death-light of Africa!
Don John of Austria
Is riding to the sea.

                                               G. K. CHESTERTON

2. More breath control exercises appear in Appendix C.

° Venice   °° A reigning French family of the time.

7 | ⟿
Resonance in Speech

We have in [the production of sound] no more
than a wonderfully flexible sound source
coupled to a wonderfully flexible resonator.

JOHN W. PIERCE, *Man's World of Sound*

THE WONDERFULLY flexible sound source of the human voice
is the vibrator called the *vocal cords*. These you can change
at will in thickness and length to produce the pitch and
timbre you want in your speech. The wonderfully flexible
resonator is a complex of vocal cavities, the mouth chamber, with the hollow pharynx at the rear and the open nostrils above, whose spaces may be coupled in or out as you
wish. How to use this resonator to the full to beautify and
strengthen your speech is what you must now learn.

Begin by finding out exactly what resonance in speech
is. The Latin word *sono* means "I sound." The word
re-sono means "I sound again." Resonance is the "sounding
again" in the chambers of the mouth, throat, or nose, elements of the tone that began in the larynx when the vocal
cords started to vibrate. Resonance adds both beauty and
strength to tone. You talk of a leading actor's resounding
speech or of his ringing tones. You·say that such-and-such
an actress has a thrilling voice, warm and compelling.
What you mean is that their speech is fully resonant. You
may notice that all the words used to describe resonance
suggest that it is both strong and pleasurable. Hence, it is
a quality you too must develop for the stage and, indeed,

for your everyday life. Resonance in one's speech is a personal as well as a professional asset.

You can identify this quality by listening to the recorded voices of actors who possess it. Such are the Caedmon recordings of nineteenth-century poetry by twentieth-century actors. The solemn themes, ornate forms, and regular meter of Victorian poetry seem to call for round, deliberate delivery. Listen to some of these readings with the text of the poem in your hand. Try the Caedmon record (TC1087) in which Sir Ralph Richardson reads the poetry of Keats. Concentrate your attention on the long vowels and diphthongs and the final ringing *n*'s and *ng*'s, as in the lines from the *Ode on Melancholy:*

> Or if thy mistress some rich anger shows,
> Emprison her soft hand, and let her rave,
> And feed deep, *deep* upon her *peerless* eyes.

> She *dwells* with Beauty—*Beauty* that must die,
> And *Joy*, whose hand is ever at his lips
> Bidding adieu; and *aching* Pleasure nigh,
> Turning to poison while the bee-mouth sips:
> *Ay*, in the very temple of Delight
> Veil'd Melancholy has her sovran shrine,
> Though seen of *none* save *him* whose *strenuous tongue*
> Can burst Joy's grape against his palate fine;
> His *soul* shall taste the sadness of her might,
> And *be among* her *cloudy* trophies *hung.*

Try reading the lines in unison with the record, matching it in speed. This will make you slow down, rather than speed up. You may find that you have to sustain some vowels and diphthongs a little longer than you usually do. You may also find that you are holding the sound almost as one holds a note in singing, keeping it reverberating in the mouth for a measurable fraction of a second. You are, in fact, resonating, or resounding, it.

When a singer holds a note, he often does so with a vibrato effect, a pulsing quality that seems to keep the tone alive, which can sometimes be heard in speech too. The earliest recorded actors—Beerbohm Tree, Julia Marlowe, Edward Sothern—used it freely. Their voices may be heard on a record called *Great Shakespearean Actors*. On the long vowels and diphthongs of important words in this record, you will hear a pronounced tremolo, almost a warble. This may sound quite affected to your ears. Although John Gielgud occasionally uses the tremolo in emotional Shakespearean passages, it has long been out of fashion. Paul Scofield, Richard Burton, Albert Finney, and Peter O'Toole, who do not use the tremolo at all, retain a clear musical ring in their speech, the characteristic resonance of the trained theatre voice.

The Acoustics of Resonance

Acoustically, the addition of resonance to tone is a phenomenon in physics. You are very familiar with the way a vase, partly filled with water, rings out simultaneously with a certain note on the piano whenever this is played. Let us suppose that the note being played is middle C. The empty part of the vase is an open-end tube of the right length to amplify one frequency among the many in the mixed tone that we call middle C. The wavelength of this frequency fits into that particular space, so that all the air in the space begins to resound with the same frequency. The tone it makes strengthens part of the tone of middle C considerably. The hollow part of the vase is now a resonator, amplifying some of the original tone. As long as the note is held on the piano, the resonator will ring, too, increasing the volume of the total sound.

Resonance in the Mouth
and Nose

Your mouth is also an open-end tube. As such, it is a resonator for the open sounds of your speech, the vowels and the diphthongs. They are all oral, sounded in the mouth. We do not usually think of them as notes of music, but actually they are very similar. Each vowel, like each note on the piano, is made up of a mixed group of frequencies. In some, like *ee*, the high frequencies dominate, making *ee* a high-pitched sound. High pitches need smaller, narrower spaces for their wavelengths; treble organ pipes are the narrowest and shortest. Accordingly, *ee* is resonated mainly in the front space of the mouth, which is made small enough by the humping of the tongue to seal off most of the mouth chamber behind and below it. By contrast, *ah* is a sound in which the low frequencies dominate. These need a larger chamber to resonate in, since their important frequencies are lower and their wavelengths longer. The tongue therefore drops when the jaw drops for *ah*. Thus, the mouth and throat are opened well, making a larger front-to-rear continuous chamber which can accommodate the long wavelengths of *ah*. Each vowel likewise has its own mouth shape, according to its peculiar resonance needs. The mouth and tongue are flexible enough to shape different amplifiers for each continuously. Only one part of the resonance system is not variable in size. This is the nose. None the less, it is the sole resonator of three most important consonants for the actor, *m*, *n*, and *ng*. Each is made when the vibrating air in the mouth is blocked by a different position of the tongue and then is released by the soft palate opening the way up into the nostrils. The powerful humming resonance of *m*, *n*, and *ng* gives additional carrying power to words which include them. They are called the *nasals*, or nasal consonants. You must be very sure to sound them well in your nose whenever they occur.

Resonance and the Lips

Careful lip shaping also tends to increase resonance. It may be that the space between the lips acts as another resonance chamber in the throat and mouth link-up. In any case, be sure to shape each vowel carefully with your lips, following the detailed descriptions in the next chapter. Check on your lip movement as you speak or read aloud by having your teacher or fellow-student observe your face in profile. Or do so yourself, standing at right angles to a mirror, using your marginal vision. Try shaping your vowels vigorously with your lips, making a rounder opening for *oo*, a more spread shape for *ee*, and a wider parting for *ah*. At once you will hear how this simple change increases the resonance of each.

Resonance and the Whole Body

The creation of resonance is a matter of holding vowel sounds for a longer time in more precisely shaped mouth openings. It is assisted too by strong inhalations such as those you worked on for breath control, and by the flexible jaw-opening movements that you acquired for projection. The recognition of resonance is a matter for your ear, but your sense of feel may assist in the process. Big resonance can be felt even when it is not heard. Deaf people can feel its vibrations when they lay their fingers on the lips of a speaker. You can feel them clearly if you will press your fingers onto the head of a fellow-student who is saying "Down, down, down!" His skull is actually ringing like a bell. It has picked up and amplified some of the variations occuring in his mouth and especially in his nose. You can feel his shoulder blades, too, vibrating like harps in the same way on the same sounds. It is very possible that every bone in the body resonates some part or other of the sounds of strong speech, helping to give them power and beauty. The firm tissues of the cheeks and chin vibrate too, as described in Group B, Exercise 4, at the end of this chapter.

Resonance and Duration

The duration of a vowel sound, as you found when reading in concert with an actor's recorded voice, is an important part of resonance. The longer a speech vowel is heard, the more it resembles a musical note. Acoustically, a long-lasting vowel tone generates as much resonance as the mouth and throat chambers can give it. If it is held only a very short time, the resonance will be less developed. Test this by saying *Oh!* as briefly as you can and then take a deep breath and say *Ohhhhhhhhh!* on one steady pitch. If you hold it long enough, you will find that you are singing *oh* rather than saying it. This singing quality is more or less developed in all the vowels and diphthongs of resonant speech.

Faults of Resonance

Four common resonance faults are stridency, hoarseness, nasality, and breathiness. If you find even a trace of one of these in your recorded speech, you must eliminate it. Exercises for the correction of each will be found in the Appendix instead of at the end of this chapter because they do not apply to every actor. The paragraphs that follow describe what each fault is and why it occurs. Study the description of the fault you suffer from, and undertake the remedial exercises for it. Continue working at them until the fault has disappeared both from your speech in daily practice periods and in casual conversation.

STRIDENCY

Strident tone is loud, shrill, and unvaried. What is said can be heard because of its loudness, but the sound is unpleasant because of a hard metallic quality. It lacks the warm ring of resonant speech. It tends to be tense and high-pitched.

This fault often develops when a young actor attempts to project his speech before he has had any technical training. Instead of taking the deep breaths which provide a strong air current for loud speech, he constricts his throat, trying to get sufficient pressure against his vocal cords from the little air already there. It works, but the strain in the tone is apparent. If this kind of projection becomes habitual, the stridency becomes habitual, too. It is unlikely to be corrected by the amateur director, because it does carry, which is more than most untrained voices do.

If your recorded speech sounds unvaryingly loud and if the nasals *m*, *n*, and *ng* are poorly sounded, you should suspect that your tone is forced. The problem will clear up quickly if you stop what you have been doing and start making tone as described in the exercises for the correction of stridency in the Appendix.

HOARSENESS

Hoarseness in speech tone is of two kinds, both dangerous to the actor. The first kind is temporary hoarseness, due to a sore throat and slight inflammation of the larynx.

If you continue to use your voice under such conditions, you may bring on acute laryngitis and total loss of your speech. This happens because the vocal cords have become inflamed. Being swollen, they cannot vibrate so as to produce tone. Absolute rest of the voice is necessary to recover from an attack of laryngitis. Steam inhalation may help, or frequent gargling with a mild salt-and-soda solution in hot water.

Repeated attacks may cause the laryngitis to become chronic. This practically disables the actor, and the disability may become permanent. The voice becomes hoarse and unpleasant at all times. Pain is absent, however, and the speaker's ears tend to get so used to his own hoarse tones that he no longer notices them. He does not realize how distressingly they strike upon the ears of others. One hoarse student who wanted to be a director insisted that he liked his speech the way it was and regarded it as his trademark! Hearing a recording of it quickly persuaded him to change his mind.

If your recorded speech tone is at all husky, or if when speaking you hear an occasional grating or scratching of the tone in the last words of a sentence, regard this with concern. It is a flaw that becomes only too apparent when speech is projected. Try to discover the cause of this huskiness. Perhaps it was abuse of the voice because of long and loud cheering at college or high school sports events. Or it may be due to excessive smoking. Or recurring attacks of laryngitis, as explained above, may be the cause. Eliminate the cause, if possible, and begin the remedial exercises for hoarseness in the Appendix, paying the greatest attention to the achievement of deep relaxation before you begin. Note that the exercises set up ideal conditions for the gentle production of soft, clear tone. These, and the relaxation series, have proved effective even with loss of voice due to polio. Work patiently through them step by step, anticipating that it may be several months or a year before your tone is normal again.

NASALITY

Nasality is the twangy quality heard on vowels which are resonated in the nose instead of in the mouth. If you suspect you have a nasal twang, listen carefully to your recorded speech, especially to words like *man, men,* or *mine,* in which there are two nasal consonants with a vowel or diphthong between them. You may also hear it on the word *now,* especially if you pronounce it *naow.*

To understand why nasality occurs, refer to Figure 6 in Chapter 4. As shown in the upper figure, the soft palate is normally held high during speech, shutting off the nose as resonator for all the sounds except the nasals *m, n,* and *ng.* Thus, to pronounce a word like *man* properly, you must lower the soft palate to sound *m* in your nose, raise it to sound *a* in your mouth, and lower it again to sound *n* in your nose. This requires great agility of the soft palate. It must act almost like a little backward-pointing tongue which stays put against the pharnygeal wall most of the time but snaps down, up, down again, in the saying of as short a word as *man.* If, however, it snaps down but once, letting the three sounds into the nose all together, the vowel *a* will be nasalized along with *m* and *n.*

Nasality may be slight or marked, according to how sluggish the action of the soft palate is. If it is marked, it may be heard in words with only one nasal consonant, such as *Andy, ten,* or *now* pronounced *naow;* it may even be heard in words without any nasal consonants, such as *I* or *how* pronounced *haow.* Any degree of nasality, however, is noticeable and disfiguring to speech and must be completely eliminated. The only time you will use it in your professional life is in a dialect such as the so-called "Yankee" speech. If you have ever asked directions in a Maine or northern New Hampshire village, you may have heard the twang. Cockney has it, but so does correct upper-class French.

Slow action of the soft palate may make speech denasal as well as nasal. This occurs because if it does not spring down to open the nasal passage quickly for *m*, *n*, and *ng*, they will sound dull and unresonant. This fault has sometimes been confused with nasality. It is corrected by the same series of exercises, with especial emphasis on prolonging the nasal consonants. Exercises for the correction of nasality are found in the Appendix.

BREATHINESS

Breathiness is a puffy or aspirate quality in speech. It is the sound of air escaping between the vocal cords when these have not been pulled together for phonation. The puff is often heard after *p*, *t*, or *k* before a following vowel. *P*ʰ*ipe* for *pipe*, *t*ʰ*ime* for *time*, *K*ʰ*ate* for *Kate* are typical breathy pronunciations. It is a wasteful way of speaking, as the breath that came puffing out in a *huh* should have been used to start the vocal cords vibrating, making a clear, resonant vowel, instead of the half-whispered one that resulted.

If you hear this whispery quality in any of the vowels of your recorded speech, undertake the exercises for correction of breathiness in the Appendix. Also do as much singing as you can. Singing tone is the antithesis of breathy tone. It helps all speech tone faults, especially breathiness. Breathiness is only appropriate for you in the theatre if your role calls upon you to utter a stage whisper.

Resonance, Singing, and Speech

If your speech has none of the faults described above, you are ready for the exercises which follow. In case you have never done much singing, spend a good deal of time on the humming exercises at first, then sing the syllables very softly but clearly. Use a pitch pipe to keep your tone true if a piano is not available. As soon as you are familiar with the sound and feel of resonance in your own speech, begin to use more of it in your everyday voice.

As the beauty and power of your speech develop, its clarity becomes more and more important. Clarity is essential to communication, and communication is your business as an actor. Clarity depends upon accurate, vigorous articulation. Good articulation and ways of achieving it is the subject of the next chapter.

Resonance Exercises

GROUP A. LISTENING FOR RESONANCE

1. Listen to all the selections on side 2 of the record *Homage to Shakespeare* (Argo, NF4, mono; ZNF4, stereo) before you identify the readers from the jacket or brochure. Decide whether each voice is that of a non-actor or of an actor. Check your conclusions with the information on the record jacket and in the brochure.

Listen again, first to the actors, then to the non-actors. Appraise the difference in resonance between the two groups. Note also any other speech differences you may have observed.

2. Listen to the voices of any two American actresses or actors on the record list. Which of the two seems more resonant? Why? Find passages in each of the two you have chosen to support your conclusion. Copy and juxtapose them on a cassette tape for confirmation.

GROUP B. EXERCISES FOR DEVELOPING RESONANCE

1A. *Sensing Resonance, a Group Exercise.* Standing in a circle, number the group around in twos—one, two, one, two, etc. Every student presses the fingertips of his right hand on his neighbor's head. First the "ones" speak the phrases below, with prolonged nasals, then the "twos." When you speak, your neighbor should feel your skull ringing like a bell. When he speaks, his should feel the same to you.

Down, down, down! No sound! The silence was profound.

Do you remember an Inn, Miranda? Do you remember an Inn?*

1B. *Humming and Moving.* These exercises help you avoid tension as singing tone is made.

    a. Do the arm-swinging transition exercise to the count of three (Chapter 5, Group D, 4). Hum on one low note for the three counts. Repeat, humming the next note up the scale for the next three counts. Continue in this way one octave up and one octave down the scale.

    b. Do the head-rolling exercise (Chapter 5, Group D, 5), singing the syllable *mah* with each repetition. Move one note up the scale with another sung *mah* each time the head-rolling direction is reversed.

    c. Do any rhythmic exercise of the upper body, such as those described below, combining it with the singing of either *mah, maw, moh, moo, mow, my, may,* or *mee,* once with each completed movement. Keep the rhythm slow. Inhale at the beginning of each movement. (Note: *mow* rhymes with *how.*)

        (1) Circling of the upper trunk, reversing direction each time.

        (2) Single arm-swinging.

        (3) Head turning, head lowering and raising, head dropping back and raising.

* From Hilaire Belloc's "Tarantella."

(4) Shoulders rounding and releasing.
(5) Hands clasping and unclasping.
(6) Arms bending and extending, sideways, upward, forward, and backward.
(7) Trunk bending sideways, and straightening.
(8) Trunk twisting sideways, and straightening.

2. *Breath Control on an Extended Singing Exercise.* Sing the following exercise, beginning on any low pitch suitable for your voice. Complete each upward series of four-note groups on one breath; snatch another breath, and sing the downward series without further inhalations. Keep the tone soft and clear and the speed fast enough to maintain an easy, bouncing rhythm. Give a light accent to the first syllable in each group by contracting the waist muscles very slightly. Otherwise, keep the waistline expanded as long as possible. Open the jaw, lips and throat well for the freest possible tone.

In the tonic sol-fa system, the tune would be do-re-mi-do, re-mi-fa-re, mi-fa-so-mi, etc. In the eight-tone octave, the intervals are one or two tones as shown by the pattern:

Ah ah ah ah, ah ah ah ah, ah ah ah ah, ah ah ah ah, ah ah ah ah, ah ah ah ah, ah ah ah ah, ah!

Ah ah ah ah, ah ah ah ah, ah ah ah ah, ah ah ah ah, ah ah ah ah, ah ah ah ah, ah ah ah ah, ah!

3. *Singing-Speaking Transition Exercise*

   a. Starting on middle C, or on any convenient pitch low in your range, sing the following series of syllables, using two breaths for the whole series, or one if possible. Repeat the series four times, moving the starting note up or down by one tone each time. Sing slowly, with full tone, and well-shaped mouth openings.

   In the tonic sol-fa system, the tune would be do-re-do, do-re-mi-re-do, do-re-mi-fa-mi-re-do, do-re-mi-fa-so-fa-mi-re-do. In the eight-tone octave, the interval

between one syllable and the next is one tone, as
shown by the pattern:

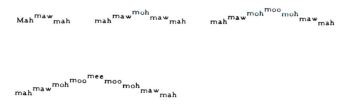

b. Sing the series below as for a.

In the tonic sol-fa system, the tune would be
do-mi-do, do-mi-so-mi-do, do-mi-so-do-so-mi-do, do-
mi-so-do-mi-do-so-mi-do. In the eight-tone octave, the
intervals are the third, fifth, and eighth tone of the
octave and the third of the octave above:

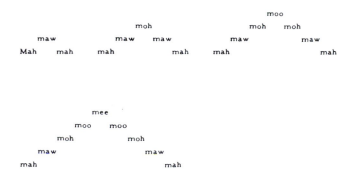

c. Sing the series as in b but use the syllables no-no-
no, no-no-no-no-no, no-no-no-no-no-no-no, no-no-no-
no-no-no-no-no-no, following the b melody exactly.

Now sing the first group only, no-no-no, and
immediately repeat it in speech, in a rising-falling
pitch pattern as much like the sung tune as possible.
Sing it again, then speak it again, making your speech
tone musical, like singing tone. Continue to alternate
for several repetitions. Then go on to the second
group, no-no-no-no-no, alternating singing and speak-

ing as before. Finally sing and speak alternately the whole *no* sequence. Take breath as needed.

d. In the same way, sing and speak alternately exercises *a* and *b* above.

e. Repeat *a, b,* and *c* above, substituting for the syllables shown one-syllable words which include a nasal consonant and a vowel or dipththong, such as *my, my, my; now, now, now; ding, ding, ding,* etc. Try each word in each exercise for variety, singing and speaking by turns.

When you judge by ear that your spoken sequences are strongly resonant, record them, listen to them, and appraise the resonance of your tone in singing and in speech.

4. *Developing Nasal Resonance*

a. Speak the vowel sequence below, to sense the quality of vowel resonance when no nasal sounds are present. Glide from one vowel to another without any cessation of tone. Watch yourself in a mirror, and match your lip-shapes with the appropriate ones in Plates IV and V. Observe that the lip opening is steadily reduced from a wide *ah* to a small, round *oo*.

When you hear strong resonance as you speak the sequences, place your fingers on your cheeks, spread out, with little fingers on the corners of your lips, and thumbs pressing up under your chin. Sense the changing vibration of each vowel. Repeat the sequence with stronger and stronger tone:

Ah . . .. aw . . . oh . . . oo!

b. Speak the syllable sequences below, in which nasal sounds have been added to the vowels. Lay fingers on your nostrils as you do so, and feel the resonance on each nasal sound. Repeat the sequences with stronger and stronger tone.

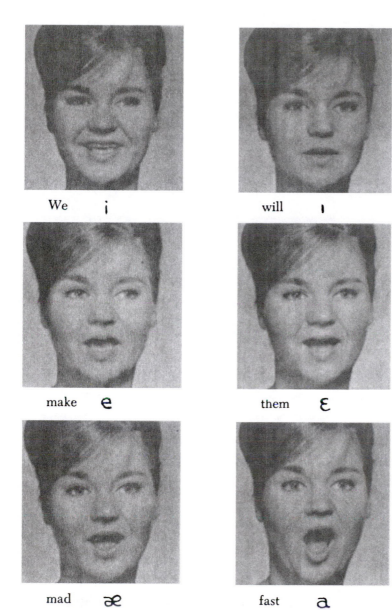

We   i   will   ɪ

make   e   them   ɛ

mad   æ   fast   a

PLATE IV. Front Vowel Sequence

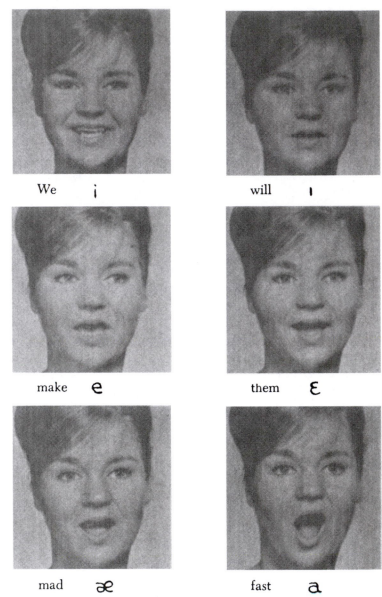

We   i   will   ɪ

make   e   them   ɛ

mad   æ   fast   a

PLATE V. Back Vowel Sequence

Mah . . . maw . . . moh . . . moo
Nah . . . naw . . . noh . . . noo
Ahng . . awng . . . ohng . . . oong
Mahn . . . mawn . . . mohn . . . moon
Mahng . . . mawng . . . mohng . . . moong
Nahng . . . nawng . . . nohng . . . noong

c. Repeat exercise *b*, using *mow, my, may, mee.* Note:
mow rhymes with *how*.

d. Speak the phrases below slowly, with full tone. Check
your resonance by pressing your fingers on your head
as you do so.

Down, down, down.
Long ago and far away.
Now and then he comes.
No sound; the silence was profound.
Once more into the breach, dear friends, once more!

5. *Combination Speaking-Moving Exercises* (This exercise
is an extension of No. 1 in this group.). Say the following phrase
sequence standing up, accompanying each repetition with a
slow outflinging of both arms from shoulder height. With each
phrase in the sequence, increase the loudness of the tone and
the breadth of the movement.

More tone!
More and more tone!
More and more and more tone!

GROUP C. READING ALOUD FOR RESONANCE

1. Read aloud in full voice the following group of poems, all
of which appeared recently in the magazine *Poetry*. Read for
both sound and meaning. Whenever it is appropriate to the
sense of the poem, prolong slightly the long vowels and diphthongs that occur in stressed syllables. Record your readings,
and listen to them, appraising the development of resonance in
your speech tone.

THE WELL

The Muse
 in her dark habit,
trim-waisted,
  wades into deep water.

The spring where she
 will fill her pitcher to the brim
wells out
 below the lake's surface, among
papyrus, where a stream
 enters the lake and is crossed
by the bridge on which I stand.

She stoops
 to gently dip and deep enough.
Her face resembles
 the face of the young actress who played
Miss Annie Sullivan, she who
 spelled the word "water" into the palm
of Helen Keller, opening
 the doors of the world.

In the baroque park,
  transformed as I neared the water
  to Valentines, a place of origin,
I stand on a bridge of one span
and see this calm act, this gathering up
 of life, of spring water

and the Muse gliding then
 in her barge without sails, without
oars or motor, across
 the dark lake, and I know
no interpretation of these mysteries
 although I know she is the Muse
and that the humble
 tributary of Roding is
one with Alpheus, the god who as a river
 flowed through the salt sea to his love's well

so that my heart leaps
 in wonder.
Cold, fresh,, deep, I feel the word water
 spelled in my left palm.

        Denise Levertov

FROM A PHOTOGRAPH

Her arms around me—child—
Around my head, hugging with her whole arms,
Whole arms as if I were a loved and native rock,
The apple in her hand,—her apple and her father,
    and my nose pressed
Hugely to the collar of her winter coat—. There
    in the photograph

It is the child who is the branch
We fall from, where would be bramble,
Brush, bramble, in the young winter
With its blowing snow she must have thought
Was ours to give her.

GEORGE OPPEN

CLEAR AIR OF OCTOBER

I can see outdoors the gold wings without birds
Flying around, and the wells of cold water
Without walls standing eighty feet up in the air.
I can feel the crickets' singing carrying them up into the sky.

I know these shadows are falling for hundreds of miles,
Crossing lawns in tiny towns, and the doors of Catholic churches;
I know the horse of darkness is riding fast to the east,
Carrying a thin man with no coat.

And I know the sun is sinking down great stairs,
Like an executioner with a great blade walking into a cellar,
And the gold animals, the lions, and the zebras, and the pheasants
Are waiting at the head of the stairs with robbers' eyes.

ROBERT BLY

2. During six months, or until you feel your resonance is fully developed, read aloud daily in the same way a group of poems of your own choice. Select them from various sources, old and new. Record and listen to them as before, listening for the increase of resonance in your tone from day to day.

3. When you habitually speak with full resonance, work daily as above from any material—poetry, prose, or drama—

which is sonorous in feeling. Check it occasionally by recording and listening to it as before.

4. The following poem works well read individually or chorally. Ring out the resonance of "change" like a warning bell.

From a poem to complement other poems

Life, if you were a match i wd light you into something beautiful,
    change, change,
for the better into a realreal together thing, change

read a change, live a change . . .
be the real people, change, . . .
know the real enemy, change, . . .

change, know the real enemy, change
change, know the real enemy,
    the real enemy,
    the realreal enemy
change your enemy
change your enemy

know the real enemy, the world's enemy
know them, know them
know them, the real enemy

change your enemy
change your
change change change your enemy
change change change change your MIND.

                                       DON L. LEE

5. More resonance exercises appear in Appendix C.

8 | ~

Articulation and
the Phonetic Alphabet

> Speak the speech, I pray you, as I pronounced
> it to you, trippingly on the tongue.
>
> SHAKESPEARE, *Hamlet*

The Speaking and Writing of Speech Sounds

HAMLET's advice to the players is as apt for actors now as it was then. Speech on the stage must be pronounced "trippingly on the tongue," that is, deftly, rapidly, easily. Most of the movements will be small; there is no need, as Hamlet pointed out, to mouth your lines like the Town Crier. But the movements must be agile, and they must be accurate. Tongue, lips, jaw, and soft palate articulate with one another, cutting up your vibrating air stream and shaping it into speech sounds.

Speech is a language we can hear. Speech in writing gives us a language we can see and read. Written speech developed when man discovered he could make pictures of what he wanted to say. Pictures led to graphic symbols for words, and then to symbols for the sound-units of words. These became the letters of the alphabet, a set of symbols for the sounds used in speech. Undoubtedly one sound originally stood for one symbol. Probably spelling was then by sounds, phonetic, easy, and consistent. But times changed. Printing was invented, and current spellings were frozen in books, by and by in dictionaries. Speech, however, was not so frozen, and went on changing from generation to generation, usually in the direction of ease of utterance. *Christ-mass* became *Christmas*, losing its *t*. The *p* in *psalm* became silent, and so did the *l*. At length English pronunciation was quite inconsistent with English spelling. Sounds were spelled with various letters, and letters stood for various sounds. *O*, for instance, spells four different sounds in the words *mother, moth, both,* and *or!*

An alphabet consistent with the sounds of speech has been invented however, the International Phonetic Alphabet, or IPA. This alphabet uses one symbol for each sound-element, or phoneme. It is the one used by Professor Higgins of *Pygmalion* and *My Fair Lady* fame, when he writes down Eliza's Cockney speech. Spelling out speech with the IPA is called *phonetic transcription*. When Professor Higgins reads aloud his phonetic transcription of what Eliza has just said, he reproduces her speech exactly. What a tool this may be for an actor! Had Higgins been one, he could have mastered for the stage any dialect or accent a role required. You can use phonetic transcription for this end, and you can also use it to discover errors of pronunciation in your own speech, a necessary step toward correcting them. Phonetic transcription is, in fact, articulating with a pencil. Knowing how to do it helps you to articulate brilliantly by allowing you to analyze difficult words and phrases into the exact sounds that compose them.

Begin by mastering the IPA. Memorize it, and use it in phonetic transcription. The section of this chapter called Phonetic Transcription and Pronunciation, which you should refer to constantly, will guide you through the difficulties you may encounter. Follow the graded exercises, which call for the transcription of individual sounds, then of nonsense syllables, then of sentences, and finally of connected speech. Simultaneously, work at the corresponding exercises in articulation. These call for practice of individual sounds and syllables, then of short verses, and so to longer patter songs, and finally to continuous passages of prose and poetry. At all times you should use your growing knowledge of sound elements to assist you in solving problems of articulation as they arise.

The consonants of the IPA largely correspond with their spelling counterparts. But the vowels and diphthongs correspond very little. The IPA uses the *a, e, i, o,* and *u* letters as symbols for the sound values they have in Italian, Spanish, or German rather than in English because the spelling-to-sound relationship is more consistent in those languages. English words in which these letters sound as they do in the phonetic alphabet are as follows:

e is the symbol for *e* as sounded in *they*
i is the symbol for *i* as sounded in *machine*
o is the symbol for *o* as sounded in *gold*
u is the symbol for *u* as sounded in *rule*
a is the symbol for *a* as sounded in in *arm*

For the other vowel sounds and for some of the consonant sounds, special symbols are used, not corresponding to any of our alphabet letters. Diphthongs are represented by the symbols of the two vowels which compose them.

Good articulation is as precise as phonetic transcription. All sounds, whether consonants, vowels, or diphthongs, are articulated on a current of outgoing breath, vibrating or not, as the case may be. If you acquired the habits of relaxation and controlled breathing during speech, as explained in Chapter IV, they will stand you in good stead as you turn your consciousness away from them and toward the careful guided articulating of the stream of sounds that make up the words you speak.

Each sound is made to differ from others by being sent out through a differently shaped mouth space. These different shapes are made by the mobile parts of the mouth, the tongue chiefly, and the jaw, lips, and soft palate, moving among and against the immobile parts, the teeth, gums, and hard palate. The mobile parts are called *articulators*. Their action is called *articulation*. In studying and practicing the articulation of sounds, you will learn to isolate one sound from all others, positioning your organs of articulation accurately so that the breath flowing through will issue in that sound, exact, clear and distinct. You will relate the articulation of each sound to its phonetic symbol,* so that knowledge of the one may reinforce knowledge of the other.

The IPA Symbols for Consonants, Vowels, and Diphthongs

Phonetic symbols for consonants each represent one consonant sound, that is, a sound in which the air is checked in some way as it passes through the mouth and then is released. This is in contrast to vowels, in which the air flows out freely as the vowel is sounded. Consonants may be grouped according to the *points of contact of the articulators* in *checking* the air. They may also be grouped according to the *action of the articulators* in *releasing* the air. Certain descriptive names, relating to

---

* It is possible that you know some of the new symbols already if you were taught to read by a modified phonetic alphabet, now in use in some forward-looking schools here and in England. It is called the ITA, or Introductory Teaching Alphabet. It uses some letters and some simplified phonetic symbols, but one symbol always represents one sound. Tests have shown that all children who learn it can read by the end of their first year, some at very high levels indeed. Later, when they are taught to read using the regular alphabet, they transfer their reading skills readily to the spellings we know. You will be doing the same thing in reverse, learning to write and spell, thereafter to read, by sounds alone.

the points of contact of the articulators, are useful as terms of reference. They appear in parentheses in the tables for consonants and vowels, in Section III below. Other terms relating to the action of the articulators are similarly explained.

Consonants may also be classified as to whether they are made with a nonvibrating or a vibrating breath current. If the former, they are called *voiceless;* if the latter, *voiced.* The vibration of the vocal cords for voiced consonants, such as *v,* can be felt if you place a finger on your larynx as you make the sound *uhvvvv!* You make unvoiced consonants, such as *f,* by passing your breath through your open glottis, your vocal cords being relaxed (see Figure 4). You will notice that *v* and *f* are a pair, made identically, except that one uses a vibrating air current, the other a nonvibrating current. Many consonants similarly exist in pairs.

Vowels fall into three groups according to whether they are made in the front, middle, or back of the mouth. (See Plates IV and V, and the Vowel Chart, Figure 7.) Diphthongs, which are blends of two vowels, are a fourth group. In the tables below, the voiced-voiceless category is not used for the vowels and diphthongs, since all are

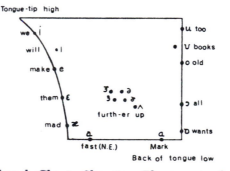

FIGURE 7. Vowel Chart, Showing Placement of the Tensed Part of the Tongue—Front, Center, or Back—for the IPA Vowels. (Adapted from Peter B. Denes and Elliot N. Pinson, *The Speech Chain,* Bell Telephone Laboratories, 1963.)

voiced. The action category is also omitted, as the articulators do not move during the emission of a vowel. For a diphthong, they glide from the position for the first vowel element to the position for the second.

Articulation and phonetic transcription make, respectively, speech you can hear and speech you can see. The tables of vowels, consonants, and diphthongs that follow show the relation of one to the other. In each table you will find, first, the sound or phoneme as you know it in a familiar word; next, its phonetic symbol; next, how it is sounded; and, finally, how it is articulated. The precise movements of the articulators and an understanding of the sounds they make thereby are your key to both standard pronunciation and clarity in your stage speech. Work through each division, starting with the sound, associating it with its symbol, and uttering it with the precise articulatory action as described. Be sure to memorize absolutely the symbol for each sound, so that one recalls the other. Refer often to three illustrations in this book, Figure 1, which shows the mouth and the organs of articulation; Plates IV and V, which show the lip-shapes for vowels; and Figure 7, the vowel chart, a schematic diagram of the mouth showing approximately where in the mouth the tongue is tensed for each vowel.

It is obvious that this knowledge will greatly assist you in the making of richly resonant tone. In Chapter 7 it was pointed out that the lips and the hollow of the mouth are specially shaped for each vowel sound, giving each its true resonance. When you study articulation, you learn exactly how to make these shapes and so to develop the resonance of each vowel to its maximum. You may experiment with how shaping helps vowel resonance by saying the sequence *oo-ah-ee*, first with scarcely any lip movement, then with lips well pursed for *oo*, opened wide for *ah*, and spread in a smile for *ee*. At once you will hear how the right shape helps to produce brilliant resonance for each vowel.

The phonetic alphabet as presented here follows Kenyon and Knott's *A Pronouncing Dictionary of American English*. For a complete discussion of American pronunciation, refer to the introductory material in that book. For British usage, refer to Daniel Jones' *An Outline of English Phonetics*. For Canadian usage, refer to both.

The Phonetic Alphabet in Sound, Symbol, and Articulation

CONSONANTS

Plosives (Table 1) are sounds made by checking the air at the point where the articulators are in contact, then releasing it with a slight explosion as the articulators part.

Table 1. Plosives

Sound	Phonetic symbol	Voiceless or voiced	Points of contact of articulators	Action by which sound is released
t as in *toe*	**t**	Voiceless	Tongue-tip is on gum-ridge (lingua-alveolar)	Plosive
d as in *doe*	**d**	Voiced		Plosive
p as in *pat*	**p**	Voiceless	Lips pressed together (bilabial)	Plosive
b as in *bat*	**b**	Voiced		Plosive
k as in *key*	**k**	Voiceless	Back of tongue pressed against soft palate (lingua-velar)	Plosive
g as in *gay*	**g**	Voiced		Plosive

Fricatives (Table 2) are sounds made by blowing a current of air through a narrow space between two articulators. The resulting sound is frictional. The *s* and *sh* pairs are called sibilant fricatives, because they have a hissing frictional quality.

Table 2. Fricatives

Sound	Phonetic symbol	Voiceless or voiced	Points of contact of articulators	Releasing action
f as in *fat*	**f**	Voiceless	Lower lip touches upper teeth ˙(labio-dental)	Fricative
v as in *vat*	**ⱴ**	Voiced		Fricative
th as in *thatch*	**θ**	Voiceless	Tongue-tip touches just-parted teeth (lingua-dental)	Fricative
th as in *that*	**ð**	Voiced		Fricative
s as in *seal*	**s**	Voiceless	Tongue-tip is pointed and grooved close to gum-ridge (lingua-alveolar)	Sibilant-fricative (hissing)
z as in *zeal*	**z**	Voiced		
sh as in *ash*	**ʃ**	Voiceless	Tongue-tip is relaxed, lower than for **s** (lingua-palatal)	Sibilant-Fricative (hushing)
z as in *azure*	**ʒ**	Voiced		
h as in *hot*	**h**	Voiceless	Glottis is partly open (glottal)	Fricative (aspirate)

Blends (Table 3) are sounds made by blending **t** with **ʃ** , **d** with **ʒ** , in one movement of the articulators.

Table 3. Blends

Sound	Phonetic symbol	Voiceless or voiced	Points of contact of articulators	Releasing action
ch as in *chip*	**tʃ**	Voiceless	Tongue-tip drops: from **t** position to **ʃ** position,	Plosive-fricative
g, j, dge, as in gyp, jip, ridge	**dʒ**	Voiced	from **d** position to **ʒ** position	

Nasals (Table 4) are sounds made to ring by using lips or tongue to block off vibrating air from escape through the mouth, and by uvula action, opening a passage for it into the nose.

Table 4. Nasals

Sound	Phonetic symbol	Voiceless or voiced	Points of contact of articulators	Releasing action
m as in *ram*	**m**	Voiced	Lips pressed together (bilabial)	Nasal: vibrating air is released
n as in *ran*	**n**	Voiced	Tongue-tip pressed on gum-ridge (lingua-alveolar)	through the nose
ng as in *rang*	**ŋ**	Voiced	Back of tongue on hard palate (lingua-velar)	

Glides (Table 5) during voicing of the air for these vowel-like sounds, the tongue moves from the position for each glide towards the position for the following vowel. If the vowel precedes the movement is from the vowel position to the glide position.

Table 5. Glides

Sound	Phonetic symbol	Voiceless or voiced	Points of contact of articulators	Releasing action
l as in *lest*	l	Voiced	Tongue-tip pressed on gum-ridge (lingua-alveolar)	Air escapes at the side of the tongue
r as in *rest* °	r	Voiced	Tongue-tip raised to mid-palate (lingua-palatal)	Air is blown over tongue, through the following vowel
y as in *yes*	j	Voiced	Tongue positioned as for the vowel i (lingua-palatal)	Air is blown through lips, and through the following vowel
w as in *west*	w	Voiced	Lips rounded, pursed (bilabial)	Air is blown through lips and through the following vowel

° *r* trilled, as in certain dialects, uses a reversed *r* symbol, ⅃

wh as in *whew!*	**hw**	Voiced	As for **w**	**h** is blown through rounded lips and through the following vowel

VOWELS

Note: All vowels and diphthongs are voiced.

Front vowels (Table 6) occur in a sequence of tongue, lip, and jaw positions. *The tongue-tip is behind the lower teeth throughout.* The front of the tongue is highest for **i** , lower and lower for succeeding vowels. The lips are slightly stretched for **i** , less and less stretched for succeeding vowels. They gradually open as the vowel sequence is pronounced. The sentence, "We will make them mad fast," uses the front vowels in a sequence, if the vowel in *fast* is pronounced half-long (see Plate IV).

Table 6. Front Vowels

Sound	Phonetic symbol	Position of articulators
ee as in *we*	**i**	Front of tongue high, lips stretched, slightly parted
i as in *will*	**ı**	Front of tongue lower than for **i** , lips less stretched, more parted
a as in *make*	**e**	Front of tongue lower than for **ı** , lips more relaxed, jaw slightly dropped
e as in *them*	**ɛ**	Front of tongue lower than for **e** , lips neutral, jaw dropped further

a as in *mad* æ Front of tongue lower than for ɛ , lips neutral, jaw still lower

a as in *fast* (half-long) ɑ Tongue on floor of mouth, slightly drawn back; jaw low

Back vowels (Table 7) occur in a sequence of tongue, lip, and jaw positions. For ɑ , the lowest, furthest-back vowel, the tongue lies on the floor of the mouth, the back of the tongue is low, the lips open, and the jaw dropped. The back of the tongue rises vowel by vowel to its high back position for the last vowel in the series, u . Likewise, the jaw rises vowel by vowel, the lips round more and more for each, until they form a close circle for the final u . The sentence, "Charles wants all old books, too," uses the back vowels in a sequence (see Plate V).

Table 7. Back Vowels

Sound	Phonetic symbol	Position of articulators
a as in *Charles*	ɑ	Back of tongue is low, tongue is relaxed, lips and jaw well opened
a as in *wants*	ɒ	Back of tongue is slightly higher, lips beginning to round (This sound is very close to the one which follows, ɔ , and is used interchangeably with it by many Americans.)
a as in *all*	ɔ	Back of tongue higher than for ɒ , lips rounder
o as in *old*	o	Back of tongue higher than for ɔ , lips round
oo as in *books*	ʊ	Back of tongue higher than for o , lips more closely rounded
oo as in *too*	u	Back of tongue in its highest position, lips tightly rounded

Mid Vowels (Table 8), starting with the highest in the mouth, are those in the phrase "further up" in American standard pronunciation. (See the Vowel Chart.) Starting with the lowest, they are those in the phrase "mother bird."

A hook called the *r-hook* is added to each of the first two, as these vowels are pronounced with a light r-coloring.

In British standard speech, the *r* is silent and the r-hook is not used. However, the final *r* in "further up" is sounded; it is called a *linking r* because it joins a final *r* to an initial vowel in the next word.

	American standard	*British standard*
further up	fɹɝ ɝ ʌp	fɜɝərʌp
mother bird	mʌɝɝ bɝd	mʌɝə bɜd

Schwa: Schwa is a name given to the unaccented vowel ə without the r-coloring, in American casual speech, the first vowel in "uh-huh." See (b) 1 below, *Vowels with the Sound of Schwa.*

ɝ , ɜ , ɚ , and ə , are in a block close together in the middle of the mouth, as shown in the Vowel Chart. ʌ is the lowest and farthest back of the mid-vowels.

Table 8. Mid-Vowels

Sound	Phonetic symbol	Position of articulators
u as in *up*	ʌ	Hump of tongue in low central position
er as in *further* (*r* sounded)	ɚ	Hump of tongue higher, more forward, vowel sound lax and light
uh as in *uh-huh*, or as in *further* (British, *r* silent)	ə ɚ	Hump of tongue slightly higher than for ɚ

ur as in *fur*, or   ʒ̆   Hump of tongue higher, more forward
further   than for ɚ , vowel sound more forceful
(*r* sounded).

ur as in *fur* or   **3**   Hump of tongue slightly lower than for
further (British,   ʒ̆
r silent)

    Diphthongs are glides from one vowel to another in the same syllable. Three diphthongs end in the vowel ɪ , three in ʊ . The diphthongs **eɪ** and **oʊ** are used interchangeably with the vowels **e** and **o** by many Americans. The diphthong forms, which are sustained, are often suitable for stage use.

    The diphthongs are heard in a sequence in the sentence, "May I join you now, Joe?"

Table 4. Diphthongs

Sound	Phonetic symbol	Position of articulators
ay as in *may*	**eɪ**	Lips and tongue glide from position for **e** to that for ɪ
ie as in *I*	**aɪ**	Lips and tongue glide from position for **a** to that for ɪ
oy as in *join*	**ɔɪ**	Lips and tongue glide from position for ɔ to that for ɪ
ew as in *you*	**ju**	Lips and tongue glide from position for **j** to that for ʊ
ow as in *now*	**aʊ**	Lips and tongue glide from position for **a** to that for ʊ
oh as in *Joe*	**oʊ**	Lips and tongue glide from position for **o** to that for ʊ

Phonetic Transcription and
Pronunciation

Transcription of speech by the phonetic alphabet is essentially spelling by sounds. Each sound is represented by a symbol. In ordinary spelling, the writer uses the letters fixed by dictionary authority as those that make up the word. In spelling by sounds, you must discard your letter-spelling habits absolutely and rely wholly on the sound of the word for the discovery of what sound units (or *phonemes*) it is made up. You must listen to it as a sound-group, analyze it into sound-units, and then write one phonetic symbol for each unit you hear. Thus, the sound-group which appears in spelling as "cat" in phonetic transcription is **k æt** . The third unit in each is identical because the third letter and the third symbol correspond in this case. Rather than relying on the occasional correspondence of symbols and letters, however, you should discard your association of word-sounds with word-spelling. You should realize that these associations are based on reading and writing, not on speech. For the spelling of speech, which is what is meant by phonetic transcription, a habit of consistent spelling by sounds, and by sounds alone, must be built up.

You must consider two kinds of problems before you begin phonetic transcription. One of these is that certain pronunciation elements which do not appear in spelling must appear in phonetic transcription. The other is that certain spelling patterns which occur very frequently do not relate to the sounds of a word and must not appear in phonetic transcription. These problems will be considered in turn.

PRONUNCIATION ELEMENTS
WHICH MUST BE TRANSCRIBED

Accent. Accent is an essential part of pronunciation, and hence of all phonetic transcription. Accent on a syllable is indicated phonetically by a vertical mark before the accented syllable: ˈæksɛntɪd ˈsɪləbl̩ If there is more than one accented syllable in a word, place the vertical mark before and *above* the syllable with the stronger, or primary, accent. Place the vertical mark before and *below* the syllable with the weaker, or secondary, accent, as in ˈwʌndɚˌfʋlɪ ˌʌndɚˈstænˌdɪŋ

Syllabication. The use of accents, as above, helps to indicate syllabication in phonetic transcription. The vowel *schwa*, ə , always indicates an unaccented syllable. Three consonants sounds, l , m , and n , are often syllables in themselves, no vowel accompanying them. In such cases, place a dot under them. Typical examples are

table:	tebl̩	broken:	brokn̩
ripple:	rɪpl̩	wooden:	wʋdn̩
chasm:	kæzm̩	roughen:	rʌfn̩
mannerism:	mænərɪzm̩	kitten:	kɪtn̩

Length. Any sound, whether vowel or consonant, which is held longer than usual, is represented by its symbol followed by a colon, ɑ: . The form lɑ:st instead of lɑst means that the vowel sound in the first is prolonged more than that in the second. The same is true when the word *cart* is pronounced kɑ:t as it sometimes is in the East, instead of kɑrt . The pronunciation rɪs: for *wrists* with the *t* omitted indicates a longer *s* than in the word *miss*, mɪs.

Pauses and Stops. A pause as long as a comma is shown with one vertical line, | a longer pause with two, || A period in continuous transcription is shown between two vertical lines, ‖ . Ordinary punctuation may also be used.

Nasality, a Pronunciation Fault. Vowels are sometimes nasalized in certain regions of the United States, particularly in the East. The result is a nasal twang. It is a very noticeable quality, invariably associated with certain dialects. In stage speech, the actor should use it deliberately as part of a dialect or not at all. Otherwise, the audience is certain to notice it as a blemish in his speech.

The phonetic symbol for nasality is a wavy line above the vowel. Use this when any trace of nasality is present in speech which is being transcribed. Examples are

man mæ̃n   men mɛ̃n   Minnie mĩnɪ

The Glottal Shock, a Pronunciation Fault. The glottal shock or click is heard in American speech as an abrupt jerk starting a short vowel, as when one says emphatically, "*A*sk me!" "*E*xcellent!" "Such *i*gnorance!" "How *u*gly!" The click occurs because the glottis snaps open instead of opening smoothly. It should be avoided except occasionally for energetic utterance. The vowel sounds harsh, and the flow of speech is broken. The phonetic symbol for the glottal shock is the query sign ʔ The instances above in IPA would be

ʔæsk mɪ ʔɛksələnt sʌtʃ ʔɪgnərəns
haʊ ʔʌglɪ

The fault may be eliminated by initiating the vowel very gently. Shape your mouth for ɛ , or for the æ of *actually*, or whatever the vowel is that you glottalize; then start to phonate it softly and easily. Practice this

many times on any short vowel that starts a sentence or
an ejaculation. If it starts a word within a sentence, join
it to the last sound of the preceding word without breaking the flow of words: "Suchignorance!" "Howugly!"

In Cockney speech, or in Glasgow regional speech, the
glottal shock is substituted for medial t in words like
little, metal, kettle. "A little metal kettle" in these dialects
would be transcribed as ə lɪʔl mɛʔl kɛʔl.

Spelling might show it as "a li-ull me-ull ke-ull."

SPELLING PATTERNS WHICH MUST NOT BE TRANSCRIBED

Vowels with the Sound of Schwa. The most difficult
sound to transcribe into phonetics is an unaccented vowel,
like those italicized in *a*loud, *e*nough, defin*i*te, c*o*ntempt,
us*u*ally. Say the words aloud, tossing them off casually.
Though the vowels in question are *a, e, i, o,* and *u,* you
probably said the words as if they were spelt uh-*loud,* uh-
nuff, def*f*-uhnit, kuhn-*tempt,* youzh-uhly. You pronounced
all the unaccented vowels alike, with a neutral *uh.* You
were correct in so doing, for all are weak syllables. To
say ay-loud, ee-nough, would be pedantic and wrong. You
will be correct also if you transcribe these vowels in
phonetics with the vowel you spoke them with, the neutral
vowel *schwa.*

It will help you to discard spelling habits during phonetic transcription of weak vowels if you also realize that
words like *the, and, of, to, as, at,* are nearly always pronounced with an *uh* sound and are spelt phonetically ðə,
ənd, əv, tə, əz, ət.   In the same way, two-
syllable and three-syllable words often are pronounced
with an ə in the unaccented syllable, as in the lists
below. Listen for this neutral vowel whenever you trans-
scribe, and always spell it with ə.

schwa spelled *a*	sofa: ˈsofə	he and I: hi ənd aɪ
	about: əˈbavt	she's at school:
	dialect: ˈdaɪəlɛkt	ʃiz ət skʊl
schwa spelled *e*	ever: ˈɛvɚ	
	(*r* sounded)	
	mother: ˈmʌðɚ	
	(*r* sounded)	
	counseling: ˈkavnsəlɪŋ	
schwa spelled *i*	pencil: ˈpɛnsəl	
	difficult: ˈdɪfəklt	
	rapidly ˈræpədlɪ	
schwa spelled *o*	conceal: kənˈsil	a cup of coffee: ə kʌp
	forget: fɚˈqɛt	əvˈkɔfɪ
schwa spelléd *u*	future: ˈfjutʃɚ	naturally: ˈnætʃərəlɪ

Capitals and Apostrophes. Do not use capital letters or apostrophes in phonetic transcription, since these have no sound quality.

He's able to do it: I can't.

hiz eblˌ tə du ɪt: aɪ kænt.

John's going to New York on Tuesday.

dʒanz qoɪŋ tə nu jɔrk an tuzdɪ.

Does Dr. Brown hold a Ph.D.?

dʌz daktɚ bravn hold ə pi etʃ di?

Silent Letters. These are so common that you may fail to realize that they are wholly absent in the sounds of words and must not appear in phonetic script:

Silent final *e*:

wake:	wek	are:	ɑr
there:	ðɛr	ale:	el
site:	saɪt	realize:	rɪəlaɪz
pure:	pjur	nature:	netʃɚ
hope:	hop	machine:	məʃin

Silent *l* before another consonant:

calm:	kɑm	folk:	fok
talk:	tɔk	polka:	pokə

Silent *p* before *s*:

psalm:	sɑm	psyche:	saɪkɪ

Consonants occasionally silent:

t in Christmas:	krɪsməs	jostle:	dʒasl̩
c in ascend:	əsɛnd		
b in bomb:	bɑm		
w in who:	hu		

Double Letters with single sounds. Many words double one consonant in spelling, in a final or medial position. The consonant is not doubled in sound, so transcribe it with one symbol only.

butter:	bʌtɚ	spell:	spɛl
happy:	hæpɪ	wholly:	holɪ
ruffle:	rʌfl̩	waggle:	wægl̩
passive:	pæsɪv	middle:	mɪdl̩

The Letter e in Prefixes and Suffixes Sounded as ɪ
or ə . Prefixes, usually unaccented, such as re-, de-, and
suffixes, such as -es, -ed, usually have the vowel sound of
ɪ . The use of ə is common also.

receive: rɪsiv rəsiv   washes: waʃɪz waʃəz
decide: dɪsaɪd dəsaɪd   decided: dɪsaɪdɪd dɪsaɪdəd
believe: bɪliv bəliv   started: startɪd startəd

Final d, in Past Tense Verbs, Sounded as t. When a
verb ends in a voiceless consonant, the final sound added
for the past tense is t, although the usual spelling suffix is
-ed.

stamped: stæmpt   latched: lætʃt
worked: wɜkt   goofed: quft
leafed: lift   wrecked: rɛkt

Final s Sounded as z. In many plurals and verb forms
ending in s, the spelled s is sounded z.

words: wɜdz   sobs: sabz
bags: bægz   comes: kʌmz
masses: mæsɪz   gives: qɪvz
roses: rozɪz   happens: hæpn̩z

Various Sounds of the Letter y. The letter y may spell
three different sounds, represented in the words transcribed
below. You must be very careful to note that the sound of
most final y's in unaccented syllables is ɪ rather than i .

yes: jɛs
by: baɪ
very: vɛrɪ

Various Sounds of the Letters c, qu, x. c spells two sounds represented in the words below. In combination with the letter *k*, it may be considered as silent. *qu* spells the sounds of **kw** , rarely of **k** . *x* spells the sounds **ks**, except when it begins a word; it is then sounded **z** .

come:	**kʌm**	quick:	**kwɪk**	axe:	**æks**
cake:	**kek**	esquire:	**ɛskwaɪr**	box:	**baks**
kick:	**kɪk**	racquet:	**rækət**	fix:	**fɪks**
ace:	**es**	xylophone:	**zaɪləfon**		
fleece:	**flis**	xenography:	**zɛnaqrafɪ**		
circle:	**sɝkl̩**	xerox:	**ziraks**		

Various spellings of the Sounds **ʃ, tʃ, dʒ** .
ʃ (sh) may be spelled by several letter combinations as shown below:

ship:	**ʃɪp**	machine:	**məʃin**
nation:	**neʃn̩**	sure:	**ʃʊr**

Spelling is very inconsistent in relation to sound with the blends **tʃ** and **dʒ** as shown below:

chirp:	**tʃɝp**	*jig:*	**dʒɪq**
fetch:	**fetʃ**	*ledge:*	**lɛdʒ**
nature:	**netʃɚ**	George:	**dʒɔrdʒ**

Pronunciation Standards for the Actor

Standard American pronunciation is the speech of most American-born actors and actresses who have reached prominence. It is the speech of the educated American, free from marked regionalisms. It is practiced by leading broadcasters on national radio and television hookups. In the case of any word in which regional variations occur, such speakers tend to use that variant which is most common and therefore familiar to the ears of the majority of their listeners. As an actor, you should accommodate your pronunciation to national standards in the same way.

Thus, if you are a Southerner, you should drop your pronunciation of I as **a** and adopt the pronunciation used by most Americans, **aɪ**. If you are a Midwesterner, you should avoid the retracted position of the tongue-tip for **r** and use a mid-position as do the majority. If you are a Bostonian and tend to pronounce *car* **ka**, using the intermediate **a**, you should change to the usual **kɑr**. If you are a New Yorker, you should avoid pronunciations like **bɔəd** for *board* and **nujɔk** for **nu jɔrk**.

You should also, however, avoid adopting the pronunciation **njʊ jɔk**. The use of **jʊ** for **ʊ**, except cept in words like *music* and *excuse* is a British variant and is used by a few Americans, but not by the majority. It is therefore inappropriate for the American stage. The so-called "stage diction," which was formerly taught in some acting schools, demanded that the student adopt this and other variants, in imitation of British usage. This practice implied that there was something inherently superior in British pronunciation. The superiority was actually not in the pronunciation of vowels but in the articulation of consonants, which in educated British speech tend to be firmer and more exact than in American. American writers such as Edward Albee use what Lee Strasberg has called the "language of speech" in contrast to the language of writing. It calls for the use of standard American vowels, familiar to all Americans and understood by most Englishmen. These vowels are appropriate for both American and British plays on the American stage, not excluding Shakespeare. Even in England, stage pronunciation varies. The language as John Gielgud speaks it is beginning to disappear. The English director Joan Littlewood rebelled vigorously against the old order when she declared in 1964, "I find the accents of Leeds, Cwm, East London and Manchester just as acceptable as those of St. John's Wood, Eton, Oxford, or hangovers from Edwardian drawingrooms."*

A safe guide to pronunciation for the American actor is Kenyon and Knott's *A Pronouncing Dictionary of the American Language,* mentioned earlier in this chapter. It lists all common English words and shows their American pronunciations in phonetic transcription. When two or more pronunciations exist for the same word, the one most widely used is given first. This is the proper one for you to use on the stage. Other pronunciations, though acceptable in the regions in which they are standard, sound strange to the majority of American listeners.

Absolute uniformity of pronunciation for actors throughout the United States is no more necessary here than it is in Great Britain. Slight differences of pronunciation do not affect communication. Rather, they add to the richness and color of speech and contribute a touch of individuality to the actor's personality. On the stage of the Canadian Stratford, British, American, and Canadian actors often appear together in the same Shakespearean production. All articulate their consonants clearly, but their vowels are not absolutely uniform. This matters not at all to the audience's enjoyment of the play.

You must keep in mind the fact that English is now becoming a world language. As such, it has national variants as well as regional and dialectal variants. Australian English, Indian English, and many varieties of African English coexist with English as we speak it. This

---

* Statement to the press, quoted by the Edinburgh *Evening News and Dispatch,* August 20, 1964.

is a situation that calls for tolerance, and the acceptance of pronunciations other than one's own as different, not as wrong.

A corollary, however, is also true. Television and radio programs in the United States, mostly produced in standard American speech, are slowly reducing the sharp variety between regional speech and standard speech. Pronunciations are learned from what is heard, and a child who listens to much standard speech on television and radio may not fully reproduce his parents' regionalisms. Thus, there may be a future fading of regionalisms and dialects into greater and greater conformity. This will be something of a loss, rather than a gain, but for other reasons than for comprehension.

Meanwhile, regionalisms and dialects are with us, and will be for a long time to come. Your business in the interests of clarity is to divest yourself of the former and to assume the latter when needed for a role.

Learning How to Do Phonetic Transcription

As a quick and simple way of learning to write from dictation using the phonetic alphabet, do the following.

1. Using a phonetic dictionary such as Kenyon and Knott's A Pronouncing Dictionary of American English, each day for five weeks, select a page beginning with a different letter of the alphabet, starting with a. Pronounce each word on the page aloud, at the same time studying it as transcribed alongside in the phonetic alphabet. Note carefully the similarities and differences in each case.

2. Cover the left-hand list of words spelled alphabetically. Look at the transcribed version of each, and pronounce it aloud. If you cannot do so, uncover the left-hand

list, and identify the word. Mark this word for further study.

3. Cover the right-hand list of phonetically transcribed words. Copy the left-hand list as spelled. Opposite each word you copy, write its phonetic transcription from memory. If you cannot recall the symbol for any sound in the word, uncover its transcribed version, and find the symbol you need. Mark the word for further study.

4. When you have finished a page, compare your transcriptions with those in the dictionary and make needed corrections. Again, mark the words in which you made errors, for further study.

5. Retranscribe all your error words, from dictation if possible.

6. Continue each day with a page of words beginning with the next letter of the alphabet.

At the end of two weeks, you should have a fair ability to transcribe nonsense syllables or single words accurately in phonetics. At the end of five weeks, you should be able to transcribe single words rapidly and accurately and to transcribe continuously from dictation at slow speed. If not, undertake another five-week stint of a-page-a-day study and copy-learning from the dictionary. Continue until you can write from dictation at moderate speed and with few errors.

Graded Exercises in Phonetic Transcription

1. Nonsense syllables, such as *tob, flig, rast* (**tɑb, flɪg , ræst**), are not words and so do not call up spelling images when pronounced. They are heard as a sequence of sounds, for each of which there is a phonetic symbol. They may therefore be transcribed readily into phonetic script.

    a. Read the following sequence of syllables aloud. Of what are these the names?

eɪ bi si di i ɛf dʒi etʃ aɪ dʒe ke
ɛl ɛm ɛn o pi kju ar ɛs ti ju vi
dʌbl̩ju ɛks waɪ zi

b. Using a single phonetic symbol, transcribe into the IPA the italicized sounds in each of the following words:

d*ay*, *b*ig, s*ee*, *d*o, *k*eep, *f*ig, *g*o, *h*ow, m*y*, *j*ay, *k*ick, *l*ow, *m*e, *n*o, *s*o, *u*p, *r*ice, t*o*, r*ue*, *v*ery, *w*ill, *y*ou, *z*igzag, h*i*ll, *e*nd, *A*nn, *au*nt, p*ar*t, *o*x (British), h*a*ll, l*oo*k, bro*th*er, o*th*er, h*ear*d, *H*erbert (*r*'s silent), *th*ink, *th*us, *sh*ow, vi*si*on, *ch*oose, si*ng*, *wh*y, m*u*se, *oh!* (sustained), n*oi*se, s*ay!* (sustained), c*ow*

2. Record the following lists of nonsense syllables on your tape recorder, speaking slowly and clearly, pronouncing them as they are spelled. (Accented syllables are italicized.) Transcribe them in phonetics from your recording as a stenographer transcribes from dictation. If you do not have a tape recorder, transcribe them from someone's dictation.

Do at least one set each week. Beginning with the second week, read aloud and record your transcription of the week before. Compare it with your original recording for accuracy.

a. sweeb, tooss, rull (to rhyme with *dull*) chig, plost, wim, fidge, sair, baw, thoot
b. grap, jerg, lums, joiv, tound, *vi*lly, *ba*zzy, *co*der, quoke, rix
c. weethe, weeth, satch, smar, hewt, mape, tawd, fow, noy, chigh (to rhyme with *high*)
d. hame, *bar*ther, *tu*dent, boh, shull, dar, *wow*li, nuck, awk, fev
e. ching, wook, *ram*boi, gew, *de*dder, fuggs, *mi*thers, hoohoo, nunch, thate (*th* as in *th*ink)

    f. bim, tobe, sass, poog, lemm, rin, vahd, zooth, rett, shup

    g. yeek, dobb (with a British *o* as in *Oxford*), hape, idge, wuz, merl, fawng, loog, sess, vith

    h. yag, slub, blued, shen, mahss, reez, flumm, herf, *eppi*, greep

    i. rast, *yacky*, *loo*muh, hahtch, trepp, munt, groob, sliv, thoodge, heesp

    j. e*loot*, skerd, thuntch (*th* as in *thus*), yerm, *zee*muh, *row*loh, blahb, wegz, joo*kay*, prann

    k. *mag*guh, *grem*ter, *smee*fuh, loobz, *is*kupp, *fladgy* (dgy as in edgy), *cow*lumm, *hoi*tuh, *rah*rah, di*zatch*

    l. koise, yohm, skewt, lerz, fime (rhymes with *time*), *gray*oh, uh-*vile*, yoodge, shoice, *how*bay

    m. tchlapp, *think*uh, sleesh, frumpt, bi*lagg*, *thirt*uh, *smog*gins, *bledgy*, *quill*ip, *sploop*uh

    n. *trow*fle, suh*loop*uh, *well*uhgitch, mat*awny*, *quoip*ing, *ler*bert, *mun*it (*mu* as in *music*), *joo*shuhboo, *loick*-ering, *ell*uhgite

    o. tri*emphal*, *roh*pid, *juke*ly, *yudd*erous, *squohmer*, *beaud*ifaw, *thoh*less (*th* as in *then*), *did*jergo, *triduhdooit*

3. *Phonetic Transcription of Colloquial Speech.* Colloquial speech tends to be spoken as a series of syllables in which an accented syllable is followed by one or two unaccented ones. The vowel in such an unaccented syllable is usually *schwa*, no matter what the spelling. The word *are*, pronounced **ar** when spoken in isolation, is reduced to a mere **ə** , when it occurs in rapid utterance, "Where are you going?" is spoken as **ˈwɛrə ju ˈgoɪŋ ?** "What are you doing?" becomes **wʌtə ju duɪŋ?** "They are here," often spelled "They're here," is spoken as **ðɛr hɪr** . Similarly, *and* is diminished to **ŋ** in phrases like **ju ŋ aɪ, hɪr ŋ ðɛr, kʌmɪŋ ŋ goɪŋ, naʊ ŋ ðɛn,** and **tade ŋ jɛstade** . *Have* and *shall* in compound verbs are heard with the vowel *schwa*. "I should have known," is usually **aɪ ʃʊd əv non.** "I shall come to-morrow," is

often **aɪ ʃəl kʌm təˈmaro** . The *h* in *him* may be silent. "Call him up," may be heard as **kɔl ɪm ʌp** *Them* is often **ðm̩** as in **aɪ sɔ ðm̩ ˈjestɚde, lets gɪv ðm̩ ə raɪd** . These variations and others like them should not be regarded as careless but rather as colloquial. Full pronunciation of vowels as spelled would result in very pedantic, unnatural speech, especially on the stage.

Transcribe in phonetics the following sentences from dictation. They should be read aloud in a rapid, colloquial style.

a. I'll come to-morrow
b. What shall I buy?
c. What have you done?
d. Tell him to wait.
e. They were swimming and diving.
f. Where's the office?
g. How's he feeling?
h. He got more and more angry.
i. Try and stop them.
j. Why are you waiting?

4. *Phonetic Transcription of Recorded Speech*
   a. Choose from your collection of recorded plays several dialogue passages and short speeches by American, Canadian, and British actors. Transcribe them in phonetics, noting differences in pronunciation of standard American, Canadian, and British speech. Read your transcriptions aloud, and record yourself doing so. Compare your readings with the originals to see if you were able to match your pronunciation with the original in each case.
   b. On the recording of *Hamlet* with Richard Burton, as produced by John Gielgud (Columbia, DOL302), are heard the voices of British, Canadian, and American actors. Listen to the recording and identify the birthplaces of as many of the cast as you can. Justify your conclusions by analyzing the pronunciation of each one phonetically.

5. *Phonetic Transcription of Careless Speech.* Daily, for several weeks, collect samples of careless speech like those following. Carry a notebook, and transcribe them as soon as heard, like Professor Higgins of *Pygmalion* and *My Fair Lady*.

1. 'wadɪdʒə wan fə dəˈsɜt ?
2. 'wʌdəjə min jə ɛnt 'qoɪn?
3. aɪ 'dɪdn̩ 'rɛkənaɪz jə.
4. təˈmarə jə kn̩ kʌm ɪf jə 'wanə.
5. lɛmɪ əˈloʊn, 'wɪljə, ɔɪ don fɪ səˈqud.
6. tɜn əˈræn soʊz ə kn̩ qɪt ə lʊk
   ætʃə.
7. wi qat 'plɛ̃nɪə tãɪm, 'plɛ̃nɪə tãɪm.
8. jə si ðɪz 'rɛlɪ 'wʌnɜfl̩ fɔrn 'muvɪz
   fə 'naɪnɪ sɛns.
9. aɪ θɪŋk ɪt 'wʌzə 'kwodɚ læst jɪɚ.
10. dʒu si əm hɪt də bɔl 'ovɚ dæt
    fɛns ?
11. wɔɪ dɪnt de tɔk tɪtˈʃʌdɚ?
12. adəˈno, 'mɛbɪ kʌz de wʌz 'mædɚ
    'sʌmθɪn.

Articulation and Pronunciation

ACCEPTABLE ASSIMILATION OF SOUNDS

Pronunciation of all consonants and vowels in each word in a phrase is not necessarily a mark of good speech. Such a habit might lead to pedantic pronunciation. Fluent speech follows what has been called the "law of economy of effort."* Continuous articulation is made easier by the

* Avery, Dorsey, and Sickles, *First Principles of Speech Training.*

blending, changing, or dropping of sounds which occur in difficult combinations. Examples are the abbreviations we use in all but the most formal speech: *don't* for *do not, won't* for *will not, didn't* for *did not.*

You must decide at what point colloquial speech becomes careless speech. While you accept the former as the norm for casual situations and for theatre speech on occasion, you should avoid careless pronunciations as a hindrance to communication. For the actor, it is appropriate only when the speech of an uneducated person is to be assumed, and even then it must not go to extremes. Except under such circumstances, his dɪdʒu   will not be   dɪdʒə , nor his ˈgoɪŋ tə gonə, nor traɪŋ tə traɪnə.

RECOGNITION AND CORRECTION OF FAULTY TONGUE-TIP SOUNDS

Corrections should be practiced both in the examples below, and in similar instances in your own speech.

1. Final *n* in an unaccented syllable:

Fault: The tongue closure for final *n* in a weak syllable may be incompletely made, or dropped, and replaced by schwa.

I hadn't spoken.	aɪ ˈhædnt ˈspokə.
There was no reason.	ðɛr wɑz no ˈrizə.
He was on a mission.	hi wɑz ɑn ə ˈmɪʃə.

Correction: Make the final n with a definite upward pressure of the tongue-tip on the gum-ridge.

2. Middle *t* or *d* in a two-syllable word.

Fault: The *t* or *d* may be dropped altogether.

I'm twenty-two.	aɪm ˈtwɛnɪ tu.
I wanted to go.	aɪ ˈwanɪd tə ɡo.
He started to do it.	hi stɑːrd tə du ɪt.

Correction: Tap the tongue vigorously on the gumridge for the middle *t* or *d*.

3. Final *t* before initial *w*.

Fault: The *t* may be dropped.

It was the only way.	ˈɪwəz ði ˈonlɪ we.
That was my fault.	ˈðæwəz maɪ fɔlt.
What was wrong?	wɑ wəz rɑŋ?

Correction: Tap the tongue for *t*, and round the lips simultaneously for *w*.

4. *l* before a consonant.

Fault: The *l* may be dropped.

Will you go?	ˈwɪju ɡo?
Please help me.	pliz hɛp mi.
Tell me the time.	ˈtɛmɪ ðə taɪm.

Correction: Lift the tongue to the gum-ridge, sound the *l*, and hold it, listening to the sound.

5. *St* followed by *st*.

Fault: The *t* of the first *st* may be dropped.

Just stop with us.   dʒʌsˈtɑp wɪθ ʌs.
I must stay with him.   aɪ mʌsˈte wɪθ hɪm.
That's the best steak.   ðæts ðə ˈbestek.

Correction: Complete the first *st* by lifting the tongue-tip from the s position to a touch for t; then drop the tongue and repeat the two-part movement for the second st.

6. *r* between two vowels when the second is *schwa*.

Fault: The schwa may be dropped and the word reduced to one syllable.

He's foreign-looking.   hiz fɔrn ˈlʊkɪŋ
We were in terror all the time.   wi wɜr ɪn tɛr: ɔl. ðə taɪm.
Look in your mirror.   lʊk ɪn jɔr mɪr:.

Correction: Be sure the tongue drops for the second vowel, and rises again to make the final *r* or other following consonant.

7. ð after s and z.

Fault: ð may be dropped.

What's the matter?   ˈwɒzə ˈmætɚ?
He was the only one.   hi wəz i ˈonlɪ wʌn.
That's the way it was.   ðæz ə we ɪt wɑz.

Correction: Practice s - ð, s - ð, using a mirror, and observing the in-out, in-out action of the tongue.

8. *t* and *d* next to *n*, in abbreviations.

Fault: *t* or *d* may be dropped before or after *n*.

I don't know.	aɪ doˈnoʊ.
He didn't leave yet.	hi dɪn liv jɛt.
I couldn't find it.	aɪ kʊn faɪn ɪt.

Correction: Practice *didn't, couldn't, shouldn't,* etc., holding the tongue on the gum-ridge for the first *d*, exploding the *n* into the nose, then releasing the final *t*.

Graded Exercises in Articulation

GROUP A. EXERCISES FOR AGILITY OF ARTICULATION

1. *The Joshua Steele Rhythm Exercises.* These exercises were invented by Joshua Steele, a noted speech teacher of the eighteenth century. Their value lies in the agility they foster in the action of the tongue. Any consonant or any combination of two or three consonants may be used in the exercises. It is done with four beats to the measure. The diagonal represents the beat, and each line represents one four-beat measure. Repeat the sound once to the beat, four times to a measure, as shown in line 1. Repeat the sound twice to the beat for line 2, three times for line 3, four times for line 4, without lessening your speed. Make the sound lightly and deftly, with a quick darting and release of the tongue. The speed must be slow at first. Beat it out with the hand or with a metronome at 72, until line 4 is very smooth and even. Then try higher speeds, until a speed of 200 can be achieved without strain or undue fatigue. Emphasize the sound that falls on the beat; the others are spoken lightly. The exercise is shown for the sound of *t*. *t* italicized must be strongly accented.

```
The rhythm:      /  (rest)  /  (rest)  /  (rest)  /  (rest)
The exercise: 1. t  (rest)  t  (rest)  t  (rest)  t  (rest)
              2. t    t,    t    t,    t    t,    t  (rest)
              3. t  t  t,   t  t  t,   t  t  t,   t  (rest)
              4. t t t t,   t t t t,   t t t t,   t  (rest)
```

Practice the excercise with single consonants and consonant clusters, as follows:

t, d, p, b, k, g
tr, dr, pr, br, kr, gr
tl, dl, pl, bl, kl, gl
tm, dm, tn, dn
str, spr, skl, spl

2. *Limericks.* Practice each limerick slowly at first. Increase the speed until you can speak one in 5 seconds, and ten in 60 seconds.

There was an old man of Nantucket,
Who kept all his gold in a bucket,
   Till his daughter, called Nan,
   Ran away with a man,
And as for the bucket, Nantucket!

ANONYMOUS

There was a young man of Cohoes
Wore tar on the end of his nose,
   When asked why he done it,
   He said for the fun it
Afforded the men of Cohoes.

ROBERT BUDETTE

Cleopatra, who thought they maligned her,
Resolved to reform and be kinder;
   "If when pettish," she said,
   "I should knock off your head,
Won't you give me some gentle reminder?"

NEWTON MACKINTOSH

There was a young man of Quebec
Who stood in the snow to his neck.
　　When they said "Are you friz?"
　　He replied, "Yes, I is,
But we don't call this cold in Quebec!"

Anonymous

There was a young lady of Niger,
Who smiled as she rode on a tiger,
　　They returned from the ride,
　　With the lady inside,
And the smile on the face of the tiger.

Anonymous

There was a young man who said "Why
Can't I look in my ear with my eye?
　　If I give my mind to it,
　　I'm sure I can do it,—
You never can tell till you try."

Anonymous

There was an old man with a beard,
Who said, "It is just as I feared,—
　　Two owls and a hen,
　　Four larks and a wren
Have all built their nests in my beard."

Edward Lear

There was an old man of Thermopylae,
Who never did anything properly,
　　But they said, "If you choose
　　To boil eggs in your shoes,
You cannot remain in Thermopylae."

Edward Lear

There was an old stupid who wrote
The verses above that we quote;
　　His want of all sense
　　Was something immense!
Which made him a person of note.

Walter Parke

There was a young poet of Japan
Wrote verses that no one could scan.
    When they told him 'twas so,
    He replied, "Yes I know,
But I like to get as many words in the last
    line as I possibly can."

ANONYMOUS

3. *Patter Songs as Listening, Singing, and Speaking Exercises.* Practice Gilbert and Sullivan's "Nightmare Songs" from *Iolanthe* (below) and "The Model of a Modern General" from *The Pirates of Penzance,* as recorded by the famous D'Oyly Carte Company on London 1215 and RCA VICS 6007 respectively. The latter is the only Martyn Green recording still listed. Green, beloved by New York and London audiences for many years in leading Gilbert-and-Sullivan roles, was the greatest of patter-song performers. In practicing, use a lip-whisper-say technique:

    a. Lip the song with the singer. Make no sound, simply articulate silently.

    b. Whisper the song with the singer.

    c. Say or sing the song with the singer.

    d. Record yourself speaking or singing with the singer.

    e. Record yourself speaking or singing the song alone.

    f. Compare your recorded song with the professional recording. Repeat the above exercises until you begin to match the original in speed and accuracy.

THE NIGHTMARE SONG

When you're lying awake with a dismal headache,
  and repose is taboo'd by anxiety,
I conceive you may use any language you choose
  to indulge in, without impropriety;
For your brain is on fire—the bedclothes conspire
  of usual slumber to plunder you;
First your counterpane goes, and uncovers your toes,
  and your sheet slips demurely from under you;
Then the blanketing tickles—you feel like mixed pickles—
  so terribly sharp is the pricking,
And you're hot, and you're cross, and you tumble and toss
  till there's nothing twixt you and the ticking.

Then the bedclothes all creep to the ground in a heap,
  and you pick 'em all up in a tangle;
Next your pillow resigns and politely declines
  to remain at its usual angle!
Well, you get some repose in the form of a doze,
  with hot eyeballs and head ever aching,
But your slumbering teems with such horrible dreams
  that you'd very much better be waking;
For you dream you are crossing the Channel, and tossing
  about in a steamer from Harwich—
Which is something between a large bathing machine
  and a very small second-class carriage—
And you're giving a treat (penny ice and cold meat)
  to a party of friends and relations—
They're a ravenous horde—and they all came on board
  at Sloane Square and South Kensington Stations.
And bound on that journey you find your attorney
  (who started that morning from Devon);
He's a bit undersized, and you don't feel surprised
  when he tells you he's only eleven.
Well, you're driving like mad with this singular lad
  (by the by, the ship's now a four-wheeler),
And you're playing round games, and he calls you bad names
  when you tell him that "ties pay the dealer,"
But this you can't stand, so you throw up your hand,
  and you find you're as cold as an icicle,
In your shirt and your socks (the black silk with gold clocks),
  crossing Salisbury Plain on a bicycle:
And he and the crew are on bicycles too—
  which they've somehow or other invested in—
And he's telling the tars all the particulars
  of a company he's interested in—
It's a scheme of devices, to get at low prices
  all goods from cough mixtures to cables
(Which tickled the sailors), by treating retailers
  as though they were all vegetables—
You get a good spadesman to plant a small tradesman
  (first take off his boots with a boot-tree),
And his legs will take root, and his fingers will shoot,
  and they'll blossom and bud like a fruit-tree—
From the greengrocer tree you get grapes and green pea,
  cauliflower, pineapple, and cranberries,
While the pastrycook plant cherry brandy will grant,
  apple puffs, and three-corners, and Banburys—
The shares are a penny, and ever so many
  are taken by Rothschild and Baring,

And just as a few are allotted to you,
  you awake with a shudder despairing—
You're a regular wreck, with a crick in your neck,
  and no wonder you snore, for your head's on the floor,
  and you've needles and pins from your soles to your shins,
  and your flesh is a-creep, for your left leg's asleep,
  and you've cramp in your toes, and a fly on your nose,
  and some fluff in your lung, and a feverish tongue,
  and a thirst that's intense, and a general sense
  that you haven't been sleeping in clover;
But the darkness has passed, and it's daylight at last,
  and the night has been long—ditto ditto my song—
  and thank goodness they're both of them over!

GROUP B. EXERCISES FOR ACCURACY OF ARTICULATION

1. *Accurate Articulation of Tongue-Tip Sounds.* Practice the sentences below with triple repetitions, lipping, whispering, and then saying them. Work for absolute accuracy. See the notes in the section on Articulation and Pronunciation in this chapter.

  a. It was included in an unannounced address.
  b. She has a sixth sense, they say.
  c. I decided to study my Latin and I started at once.
  d. I couldn't decide what I wanted to do: I wanted to go, but I wanted to stay, too.
  e. Sidney should show up soon, shouldn't he?
  f. I'll just stop for my shoes at this shoestore.
  g. It was a rural line, and I didn't wait for a return phone call; the connection was broken.
  h. Did you get that pretty little kitty at the pet store?
  i. This university must develop a summer theatre of some kind.
  j. The Leith police dismisseth us, said the Quakers.

2. *Accurate Articulation of Colloquial Speech.*
  a. Below are colloquial speech samples transcribed in phonetics, showing errors as heard in conversation. Practice them, correcting the errors but maintaining an informal style.

(1) I told him I wouldn't go.

aɪˈtolm̩ aɪ ˈwʊdn̩ qo.

(2) Everybody's reading "Elmer Gantry."

ˈɛvɪˌbadiz ˈridɪn ˈɛmɚ ˈqæntri.

(3) I didn't eat breakfast this morning; it's my new diet.

aɪ dɪnɪt ˈbrɛfəs: ˈmɔrnɪn;
smaɪ nu daɪt.

(4) Do you realize we've been sitting here an hour and a half?

dʒə ˈrɪəlaɪz wiv bɪn ˈsɪtn̩
hɪr ˈnawɝnə hæf?

(5) What have you got for lunch? I've got a salmon and tuna sandwich.

wʌtʃɚ qʌt fə lʌntʃ? aɪˈqʌtə
sẽːəmn̩ n̩ tunə sæmwatʃ.

(6) I don't understand how a car like that can be worth twelve thousand dollars.

aɪ dʌnt ˈʌnəstæn hav ə ka laɪk
ðæt kɪn bɪ wɝθ twɛlv ˈθazɪn ˈdʌlɚz.

(7) Excuse me, let me out of the elevator. Would you please move?

skuz mi, ˈlɛmɪ ˈavtə ðə ˈɛləvetɚ.
ˈwʊdʒə pliz muv?

(8) You can't use the washing machine, it's out of order tonight.

jə kɪnt juz ə'wɔrʃɪŋ ʃɪn, 'sævdə 'ɔrdə tə'naɪt.

(9) Who's the man with the funny-looking hat? He must be a foreigner.

huz ə mæn'wɪθə 'fʌnɪ'lukɪn hæt? hi mʌs bi ə 'fɔrnɚ.

(10) I told you they didn't serve breakfast after nine o'clock.

aɪ 'todʒə ðe dɪn sɝv 'brɛfəs 'æftɚ naɪn ə'klak.

(11) If we don't have rehearsal tomorrow night, I'm going to get a ride down to New York and see my honey.

ɪf wi don æv 'rɝzl tə'mʌrə naɪ, 'ʌmɡʌnə 'qɪtə 'raɪdæʊn tə nə'jakn si maɪ 'hʌnɪ.

(12) That's what I mean, I'm only nineteen.

ðæz hwa aɪ min, m̩onɪ 'naɪtin.

(13) Ring up an item for me, two-twenty-five and twenty-ninety, and give me a total.

rɪŋ 'ʌpn̩ 'aɪdm̩ fɚ mi, 'tuʔwɛnɪ 'faɪvn̩ 'twenɪ 'naɪnɪn 'qɪmɪə 'todl̩.

(14) I'm afraid this cracked mirror will break.

aɪm fred ðɪs krækt 'mɝəl brek.

b. Make your own collection of 100 sentences of this kind and practice them, using two phonetic transcriptions. The first should show the original errors. The second should show how you corrected them, retaining easy colloquial pronunciation, as in the example below.

Did you eat yet? No, did you?

dʒit dʒɛt ? no, dʒu ?

dɪd ju iʈ jɛʈ ? no, dɪdʒu ?

3. *Exercises for Especially Rapid, Free Articulation.* Read "Jim" as a class exercise. Sitting in a circle, read around rapidly, one or more lines apiece, with unbroken rhythm. Use deft articulation, rapid pace, and bouncing mock-serious inflections. Time your readings, working for increase of speed without loss of clarity.

You may also use "Jim" as an individual exercise for colloquial clarity.

JIM
WHO RAN AWAY FROM HIS NURSE AND WAS EATEN BY A LION

There was a Boy whose name was Jim;
His Friends were very good to him.
They gave him Tea, and Cakes, and Jam,
And slices of delicious Ham,
And Chocolate with pink inside,
And little Tricycles to ride,
And read him Stories through and through,
And even took him to the Zoo—
But there it was the dreadful Fate
Befell him, which I now relate.

You know—at least you *ought* to know,
For I have often told you so—
That Children never are allowed
To leave their Nurses in a Crowd;
Now this was Jim's especial Foible,
He ran away when he was able,
And on this inauspicious day

He slipped his hand and ran away!
He hadn't gone a yard when—
                              Bang!
With open jaws, a Lion sprang,
And hungrily began to eat
The Boy; beginning at his feet.

Now just imagine how it feels
When first your toes and then your heels,
And then by gradual degrees,
Your shins and ankles, calves and knees,
Are eaten slowly, bit by bit.
No wonder Jim detested it!
No wonder that he shouted "Hi!"
The Honest Keeper heard his cry,
Though very fat, he almost ran
To help the little gentleman.
"Ponto!" he ordered as he came
(For Ponto was the Lion's name),
"Ponto!" he cried, with angry frown,
"Let go, Sir! Down, Sir! Put it down!"

The Lion made a sudden Stop.
He let the Dainty Morsel drop
And slunk reluctant to his cage,
Snarling with Disappointed Rage,
But when he bent him over Jim,
The Honest Keeper's Eyes were dim.
The Lion having reached his Head,
The Miserable Boy was dead!

When nurse informed his Parents, they
Were more Concerned than I can say—
His Mother, as She dried her eyes,
Said, "Well, it gives me no surprise,
He would not do as he was told!"
His Father, who was self-controlled,
Bade all the children round attend
To James's miserable end,
And always keep a-hold of Nurse
For fear of finding something worse.

HILAIRE BELLOC

4. *For energetic articulation.* Try a game: lip a line from the following poem in silence; let the class try to *see* which it is.

THE FIRST EIGHT DAYS OF THE BEARD

1. A page of exclamation points.
2. A class of cadets at attention.
3. A school of eels.
4. Standing commuters.
5. A bed of nails for the swami.
6. Flagpoles of unknown countries.
7. Centipedes resting on their laurels.
8. The toenails of the face.

JANE KENYON

5. *For casual clarity.* With good articulation established, read the following conversationally.

SKUNK

On the back lawn tonight a skunk, shyly
aggressive, approached the screened-in porch for one
good look, I like to think, at the resident poet.

I told him, tentatively, my life's goal; to end
up blaming no one but myself for anything
I didn't do—my definition of a happy man.

He didn't flinch. If my instinct for audience
response is what I think it is, he listened,
then lumbered off towards the yard's one tamarack

like a monk who's had enough of wise advice
to last one lifetime, or like a meek apprentice
hoping his own idea might still occur.

GARY MIRANDA

6. *For Mastery of Difficult Consonant Combinations.* Listen to George Irving's *Tongue Twisters* (Caedmon TC 1432). Write out the series, then join him in speaking it, trying to match him in speed and agility. Record yourself, noting any errors you make, and correct them by slowly going over the hard bits, as a musician practices difficult bars of music, until you can say them fluently.

7. More articulation exercises appear in Appendix C.

9 | ~

Variety in Speech:
Pitch, Rate, and Stress

> . . . it was the kind of voice that the ear fol-
> lows up and down, as if each speech is an
> arrangement of notes that will never be played
> again.
>
> F. Scott Fitzgerald, *The Great Gatsby*

In the quotation above, a writer senses the profound
emotional effect of melodious inflection on the hearer. The
speech is varied, hence expressive. Pitch, rate, and stress
are the three elements which may give a speaking voice
infinite flexibility, corresponding in some degree to melody,
tempo, and accent in music. Speech pitch, in fact, varies
with the same muscular movements that vary musical
pitch. Speech rate, like tempo, may be faster or slower
according to the mood of the piece and the interpretation
of the performer. Speech stress, like accent in music, high-
lights a special word or phrase.

Lack of these elements, by the same token, makes a
voice monotonous. It has been said that the nature of
attention is to wander. If this is true, you can hold the
attention of your listeners only by diverting it from time
to time. If your speech is marked by monotony of pitch,
evenness of rate, and unvarying stress, it offers no di-
versions to the hearer. His attention quickly wanes, no
matter how good his intentions, nor how interesting the

material in itself. Monotony is a handicap in any speech, most of all in an actor's.

Pitch as an Element of Variety in Speech

A ranging speech pitch, carrying words now high, now low, is an admirable attention-getter. In addition, it makes meanings clear. The statement "I shall go," pronounced with a positive downward inflection, is a clear statement of intention. Pronounced with a high-pitched *shall*, it declares action in the face of opposition. Pronounced with a high-pitched *I*, it implies that I, not someone else, shall go. Pitch-change also carries with it strong overtones of emotion, high pitch suggesting rage or fear, low pitch calmness and confidence. As an actor, you should employ a great range of speaking pitch, from high to low, through as much as two octaves, to meet the varying needs of a scene.

Your voice at present may possess only a very narrow range of speech pitch, corresponding to perhaps eight or ten successive tones in the musical scale. Before attempting to increase this range, you must understand the physiological basis of pitch change in speech. Next, you must develop sensitivity to the rise and fall of speech pitch in the voices of others. Then you should undertake the exercises for developing pitch range in this chapter. Finally, you should make a conscious effort to speak in ordinary conversation as well as in public with an expanded range of speech pitch, so that you may speak on the stage with the naturalness and vigor of vivid conversational inflections.

Change in speech pitch, like change in the pitch of a sung note, depends upon changes in the vocal cords, which cause tone when they vibrate. The mass and tension of the vocal cords may be varied by muscles which pull upon them when we will to change pitch. If the mass becomes greater and the tension less, the pitch given out by the vibrating cords, as from a loosened violin string, is lower. If the tension is increased, the tightened cords become thinner, losing mass per unit of length. The resulting pitch will be higher.

These changes are directed by the ear, which is a vital part of the singing and speaking mechanism. The muscle movements of pitch change are almost imperceptible kinasthetically. They signify their occurrence through the ear; the singer hears the pitch of the note he sang returning to his own ears and recognizes it as the one he intended. Thus, as a child, you learned to match tones by listening to yourself through this built-in feedback system, comparing your own sung note with the note you were matching, correcting yourself as necessary. This sense of pitch discrimination develops earlier in life for some, later for others. Its development is too often hindered by singing teachers in elementary schools, who tell a child that he is a "listener," or a "monotone," meaning that he is tone-deaf. They may even request him not to sing with the others, thereby doing him a great wrong. The slow reader is not denied practice in reading because his reading readiness is behind that of his classmates. Likewise, the child slow to learn to carry a tune should be encouraged, not silenced. Pitch readiness, like reading readiness, almost always develops in the course of time if it is given a chance.

Singing tone and speech tone are alike in that the vowels and the continuant consonants of speech always occur momentarily in a certain musical pitch. They are different in two ways. First, the extreme brevity of speech sounds minimizes their musical quality. Second, they do not usually remain in one pitch but often slide up and down from it. Speech pitch is characterized by slides, whereas musical pitch moves in leaps. These leaps are exact, in accordance with the fixed frequencies of the tones of the scale. Speech slides are free. Any word may slide up or down on its vowel or continuant consonant, as in WE-ll!, or may even use a circumflex inflection, as in OoOOoh!. The important fact is that the correspondence between speech pitch and musical pitch in a spoken vowel is normally of momentary duration. This duration may be lengthened when the speaker wishes. Intoning is an instance of lengthened duration of speech vowels, bringing them close to sung vowels in quality.

The relationship of resonance to pitch must be briefly considered here. Certain vowels are not easy to utter in a high pitch because the frequency range of the mouth shape and pharynx-shape by which they are made may itself be low. This is the case especially with the vowel ʊ . In general, the round back vowels in *ma, maw, mow,* and *moo,* according to Alexander Wood in *The Physics of Music,*° are made with mouth and pharynx shapes in which the lower frequencies are more prominent. For each shorter vowel in the series *mat, met, mate, meet,* two frequencies are prominent, one high and one low, Speech may, and sometimes does, force vowels out of their natural frequencies under stress of emotion. But the quality of the tone is likely to be impaired.

Keeping the vocal tract relaxed makes it possible, however, for you to maintain resonance under difficult conditions such as these. A steady, full breath stream likewise will improve your resonance at both higher and lower speech pitches. Each of the techniques of speech, in fact, as you master it, assists the other to function more perfectly.

This chapter includes both pitch-writing and pitch-speaking exercises. These should be carried on concurrently as growing pitch discrimination in your ear helps you to control pitch changes in your vocal cords. You must try to develop both together. The exercises require

° New York, Dover, 1944.

both the reading and writing of sentences using pitch transcription. This is a way of showing graphically how inflections rise and fall like notes in a melody. Dots are used instead of notes and are arranged on a musical staff according to the pitch of each syllable. A simple example is below.

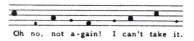

Oh no, not a-gain! I can't take it.

This shows rises and falls in speech pitch. Slides may be shown by commas up and down.

Oh no, not a-gain! I can't take it.

This method will be used in the pitch-study exercises at the end of the chapter.

One of the exercises presents passages from *Henry VI*, *Lear*, and *Hamlet*, transcribed from recordings by John Barrymore, John Gielgud, and Richard Burton. Remarkable differences of pitch range characterize the readings, and these are apparent in the pitch transcriptions. You should follow these transcriptions while listening to the records. You may yourself rehearse the same lines, then note down each reading in pitch transcription, record it, and compare your recording with the others. Slavish imitation of another actor's interpretation is, of course, never to be part of a performance. But as a means of urging you to go beyond your former limits of pitch use, comparison of this kind may serve a useful purpose.

During the period when you are breaking away from a limited pitch range, it may help you to use pitch transcription as a means of planning definite pitch inflections which you will use for a practice poem or speech. You may use any or all of the selections in the exercises. Your first draft in pitch transcription may dissatisfy you as you read it aloud, and you may need to try out several revisions of your inflection patterns before you are satisfied. Eventually you should present the selection with inflections as they satisfy you, for comment and appraisal by your teacher or fellow actors.

These exercises will quickly strengthen your discrimination of speech pitch. You must now train yourself to be able to produce as wide a range of speech tones as your voice will permit. The pitch-development exercises for this purpose begin with singing exercises and continue with a speech-singing transition group which is both difficult and important. It may be extremely hard for you to escape from lifelong habits of minimal pitch change in speech inflection. If you will give intense attention to matching a speech series to a sung series, note by note, playing the latter on the piano if necessary, you may finally achieve much higher and lower levels of speech pitch than formerly. When you have managed to use these new pitch levels in the various number sequences, you will find it possible to use them in short sentences, as guided by the exercises. Constant repetition takes away the strangeness of hearing your own speech tones above or below their previous pitch range. When you speak lines of powerful poetry, taking the next step, you will naturally use vivid inflections and so will carry the process further. You may alternate this with listening to poetry readings on records as suggested. Gradually your ear will become more and more familiar with the use of a wide pitch range in interpretation. Eventually, you will begin to use your new range in vigorous conversation, without conscious effort. You will then be confirmed in new habits of freer, fuller inflections. These will hereafter be available to you as an actor.

Repetitive inflections are a serious fault in an actor's voice. You may fall into this fault when you are reading verse, especially blank verse such as Shakespeare's. Carefully avoid reading a line down, with a falling inflection on the last syllable. This tendency corresponds to a conversational habit of beginning a sentence at a normal pitch, gradually dropping lower and lower as the breath supply diminishes until the sentence ends on a low-pitched barely-audible syllable. The effect is one of weakness. Your ear must always be listening for, recognizing, and avoiding this dreary speech cadence. Special examples for working to correct this fault will be found in the next chapter, in the exercises based on the reading of Shakespeare.

Rate as an Element of Variety in Speech

Change in speech rate, the second element in variety, is much easier to achieve than change in speech pitch. "In speech," says S. J. Campanella, an electrical engineer specializing in communications systems analysis, "a human utilizes approximately forty basic sounds, and produces them at an average rate of ten per second." You can produce more or less quite easily, and your increase or decrease in rate as you read a passage can be measured in minutes or seconds. Both faster and slower speech on the stage have their problems, and these will be considered in turn.

Extremely rapid speech is often needed in humorous scenes, or in scenes of rising excitement. The problem is not merely to utter the words at a fast rate but to utter them clearly and intelligibily as well. Even a minor degree of faulty articulation will interfere with your audience's understanding of your rapid speech on the stage.

The problem of increased speed is the problem of moving the articulators rapidly, smoothly, and accurately through the minimum distances compatible with the making of clear speech sounds. Thus, a good *i* sound can be made with the lips well stretched laterally; it can also be made with a lip-stretch very slightly greater than for *ı* . A t can be made with a hard thrust of the tongue-tip to the gum-ridge or a light delicate touch on the same spot. What the actor must aim for in rapid speech is a sequence of infinitely small, accurate movements flowing in a fast rhythm without a pause except where the sense pauses. The tongue especially glides like an acrobat through everchanging positions without apparent effort, coming to rest easily when the sentence or thought is finished, to leap out again instantly for the next series of movements. Precision and control are the keywords.

To speak slowly, on the other hand, might seem to be an easy task. Certainly there is plenty of time for all the necessary movements. The problem here is not mechanical; rather, it is psychological. When you must read a solemn, sonorous passage, you may feel self-conscious as you slow down your speech rate. You are not used to speaking deliberately and inflecting richly. If you are afraid to enlarge your pitch range as you lengthen your vowels and continuants, you may become merely monotonous. If you fear that you are manipulating your speech simply for a richer effect, your self-consciousness may increase. You may find it harder to speak slowly than to speak quickly.

With both fast and slow speed, the timing of your breathing is important. In rapid speech, the great numbers of consonants you pour out in a single second require frequent replenishing of breath. Breathe deeply and quickly at your moments of pause, referring back to Chapter 6 for this technique. Likewise, for slow speech you will need ample breath for the prolonged vowels. In both cases, find places when you may inhale so as to replenish the breath supply fully and in good time.

Among the records suggested for your record collection in Chapter 1 is that of Richard Burton reading the poetry of Thomas Hardy (Caedmon, TC1140). Listen to it, and note how slow the pace sometimes is. Read the Hardy poems yourself, and compare your time span for each with that of Burton. If you are faster than he, slow your reading both by lengthening the pauses and by increasing the time duration of vowels, diphthongs, and continuant consonants in stressed words. If you feel awkward in doing so, recall that the great ballet dancer Nijinsky replied, when he was asked how he carried out his extraordinary prolonged leaps, "It is only necessary to pause a little in the air." You will learn to pause a little within the word, strengthening its impact on your hearers.

When you feel comfortable in reading poetry slowly, you may use the same method with slow passages from recorded plays. You should remember that in matching your models, you are really only getting accustomed to the use of a wider range of speech speeds.

The ultimate skill in achieving variety of rate permits the actor to speed up or slow down as his lines suggest, never maintaining the same speed for very long. Evenness of pace is as great a cause of monotony as evenness of pitch, and you must take pains to avoid it. Sudden bursts of rising speed and rising pitch, especially if your articulation is flawless, may have an electrifying effect upon an audience. Similarly a slower and slower rate of speech may enhance and deepen the listener's mood of awe and wonder.

Stress as an Element of Variety in Speech

Stress is a close and natural ally of pitch and speed in the development of variety in speech. Stress may be light or heavy, as a word is whispered or shouted. The handling of both these extreme effects of stress has already been dealt with in Chapter 6, on breath control. It remains to consider how to develop the ability to use the many fine degrees of varying stress which lie between.

Increased stress on a word is the result of increased pressure of the breath on the vocal cords, with increased amplitude of the sound waves of speech. The effect on the listener's ear is one of greater loudness or force, or both together. The simplest example of stress use is in the two-syllable word, which normally has one syllable stressed or accented and one unstressed or unaccented. The stressed syllable is usually the first, as in such common words as water, mother, summer. In short three-syllable phrases, there is normally one stressed syllable: Good morning, Where are you? I don't know. Don't you see? Ordinary speech is characterized by a pleasant rippling rhythm of stressed and unstressed syllables, as in the following: Do you know what time it is? What's the matter with you? I'm going to be late today, I'm afraid. He wants us to finish this tonight. One stressed syllable out of three is a common pattern of English speech. These syllables are usually those that are important to the meaning.

Herein lies the clue to your use of stronger stresses on the stage. In the first place, all your speech from the stage must be uttered with sufficient force to permit the audience to hear it readily. Sometimes you must give an additional measure of force to a plot line. You must often do this subtly, delicately increasing the breath pressure above the safe minimum for projection so that the line appears to be spoken casually. This skill with stress dynamics is akin to the sense of touch on the piano. A good musician does not pound the keys nor a good actor his syllables. With restraint and control, he propels the significant word with just enough force and not too much. He knows that pitch, speed, and force normally rise and fall together and will reinforce each other when climactic effects must be created. On the other hand, there is a compelling strangeness about a word spoken low and loud, as there is about one which is high and soft. The unexpectedness of these gives them special dramatic power.

The stress exercises in this chapter begin with four in which the technique for increasing or decreasing *stress* on a word is isolated from its associates, change in *pitch* and *speed*. The technique is a refinement of that used in the exercises on breath control when a shriek or scream must be uttered on the stage. You are seeking to gain control over the amount of force you will use to get the effect required by dramatic need. It will soon become apparent to you that it is almost impossible to alter stress in a word without a change in pitch or speed or both. Begin to use them all together. Depend upon your techniques of relaxation and breath control to permit you to do so. In the final exercise of the series, your control of pitch, speed, and rate should give your speech a flexibility that will permit it to do the utmost bidding of your creative imagination as you work on a role.

From now on you should continue to listen to records, noting how the elements of variety are used simultaneously or alone. Listening repeatedly to a consummate artist like Sir John Gielgud, in his program of Shakespeare readings *Ages of Man* (Caedmon, SRS 200), you may discern beneath the powerful theatrical effect the means used to achieve it, the infinite graduations of pitch, speed, and stress by which the words were made to come alive and move an audience to tears and laughter. "The recorded voice of John Gielgud," says Goddard Lieberson, president of Columbia Records, "which engages only our sense of hearing, shows us at once his unique quality for conveying the most profound emotions with a vocal skill we might expect from a trained singer. In this sense he is a musician, bringing to his performances the subtleties of such musical ingredients as the fortissimo, pianissimo, crescendo, or diminuendo. And just as a musician seeks the secret meanings of Beethoven, so Sir John, in this case, has taken Shakespeare for his repertoire."

Gielgud's *Ages of Man* is a solo performance. Your reading of lines, on the other hand, must be related to the interpretations of your fellow actors. As a play is rehearsed, you will try out many readings for each important line. One or another of these will not necessarily be right or wrong but will be nearer or further off from what the director and the cast together are seeking, the inner spirit of the play. As the work proceeds, a new inflection may suggest itself to you, or a new pace may be set for a passage to meet the needs of a developing scene. You will not permit your line readings to become set either as to inflection, rate or stress while new directions of mood and meaning may still offer themselves in rehearsal. Finally, however, if all goes well, the work of the actors, the director, and the scene designer will engender a living entity, the play in performance. Line readings will now be constant except as they change slightly to suit the mood of the audiences in their varying receptions of the play.

When a successful Broadway play has settled into its run, it is time to record it. Thereafter, those who have seen the performance will be able to recreate the entire experience from the record as speech after speech recalls each scene. For those who did not see it, there may well be a sense of presence as the voices of actors answering one another bring the imagined action of the play vividly before the mind's eye and ear. Such skill in communication is possible to the actor who learns to control creatively those interpreters of meaning—the pitch, rate, and stress of his speech on the stage. These elements, always in demand for an actor, are never more important than in the speaking of Shakespeare. This is the subject of the next chapter.

Exercises for Variety of Pitch, Speed, and Stress in Speech

GENERAL DIRECTIONS: Conscious manipulation of pitch, speed and stress is a necessary part of the exercises which follow. Any artificiality of result at first need not give you concern, since you are practicing a technique, not performing. Mastery of the technique leads eventually to complete freedom of interpretation.

GROUP A. LEARNING PITCH TRANSCRIPTION OF SPEECH INFLECTIONS

DIRECTIONS: Pitch transcription shows speech inflections set up on music staff paper but uses dots instead of notes. Each syllable is shown by one dot, a large dot for a stressed syllable, a small dot for an unstressed one. The position of the dots on the staff suggests the pitch of the spoken word, high or low. Dots on the middle of the staff are in the middle of the speaker's range. Extremely high- or low-pitched words may be shown by dots placed on lines or spaces above or below the staff, as in music. Commas may be added to dots to show pitch slides up or down. The representation is approximate rather than exact. Its purpose is to suggest to a reader the speech melody of the words as spoken.

1. *Reading a Conversation in Pitch Transcription.* Below is a conversation with its inflections shown in pitch transcription. Read it aloud, moving your speech pitch up and down to follow the rise and fall of the inflection. Record it, play it back, and compare it with the transcription.

2. *Reading Pitch Transcriptions of Sentence Inflections.* Read the sentences below, following the inflections as shown.

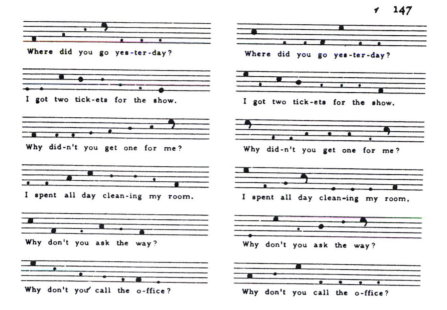

3. *Writing Pitch Transcriptions of Sentence Inflections.*
Using music staff paper, write appropriate inflections for the
sentences in the exercise Accurate Articulation of Colloquial
Speech, Chapter 8.

4. *Transcribing Inflections from Recorded Speech.* The sentences below were transcribed from Brian Hooker's translation
of Edmond Rostand's *Cyrano de Bergerac*, as spoken by José
Ferrer (Capitol, W283). The steps in making such a transcription are as follows:

   a. Transcribe sentence by sentence. Write out a sentence
   below a staff, dividing the syllables. Set its pitch
   boundaries by listening to it, picking out its highest
   and lowest pitched words, and dotting them in on
   the staff.

   b. Listening again, dot in the other syllables on the
   appropriate lines.

   c. Listen again; mark the stressed syllables by large dots.

   d. Listen again, and add pitch slides where you hear
   them.

   e. Reproduce the inflection by reading the sentence
   aloud. Correct the transcription as needed.

Familiar: Well, old torch-light, hang your hat ov-er that chand-e-lier,

it hurts my eyes!

El-o-quent: When it blows, the ty-phoon howls, and the clouds dark-en.

Dram-a-tic: When it bleeds, the Red Sea.

En-ter-pri-sing: What a sign for a per-fum-er!

Transcribe the entire Nose speech from the same play, as spoken by Sir Ralph Richardson on Caedmon, TRS 306.

5. *Reading Pitch Transcriptions from Shakespearean Recordings.* The following are transcriptions of speeches from Shakespeare as recorded by John Barrymore, John Gielgud, and Richard Burton, on the records listed. Read them aloud as transcribed. Try to encompass with your own inflections the great pitch builds and leaps that occur in each one. Listen to the whole of the records from which these were taken. Listen also to other recordings of the same plays, and transcribe these speeches from them for purposes of comparison.

Henry VI, III, ii, as read by John Barrymore
(Audio Rarities, Vol. I, 2280)

I'll make my heav'n to dream up-on the crown...

And from that tor-ment I will free my-self

Or hew my way out with a blood-y axe!

Why, I can smile, and mur-der while I smile,

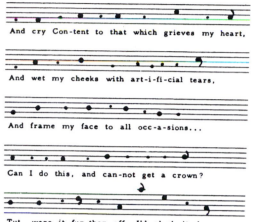

And cry Con-tent to that which grieves my heart,

And wet my cheeks with art-i-fi-cial tears,

And frame my face to all occ-a-sions...

Can I do this, and can-not get a crown?

Tut, were it fur-ther off, I'd pluck it down.

King Lear, V, iii, as read by John Gielgud on Ages of Man

(Columbia, OL 5390)

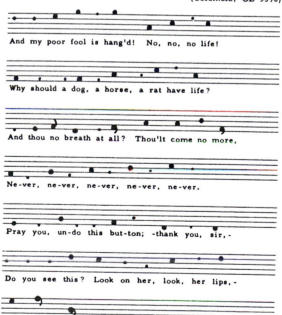

And my poor fool is hang'd! No, no, no life!

Why should a dog, a horse, a rat have life?

And thou no breath at all? Thou'lt come no more,

Ne-ver, ne-ver, ne-ver, ne-ver, ne-ver.

Pray you, un-do this but-ton; -thank you, sir,-

Do you see this? Look on her, look, her lips,-

Look there, look there!...

6. *Collecting Casual Inflections.* Daily, for several weeks, collect samples of strongly inflected short sentences from casual conversations you overhear. Write out the inflections in pitch transcription. Each day, read aloud the ones you transcribed the previous day. Work with a partner, if possible, reading his transcriptions and letting him read yours, so that you may check their accuracy. You may combine this exercise with No. 5, Graded Exercises in Phonetic Transcription, Chapter 8, writing the words of the sentence in IPA under the pitch transcription.

GROUP B. EXERCISES FOR DEVELOPING VARIETY OF
SPEECH PITCH

DIRECTIONS: Do the first part of the Actor's Warm-up Series
in preparation for the following.

1. *Singing through an Octave on Ah, and on a Number
Sequence.* Starting at a low pitch easy for you, sing slowly up
and down one octave on *Ah!* Repeat, but sing the numbers *one,
two, three, four, five, six, seven, eight,* up and down through
the same octave.

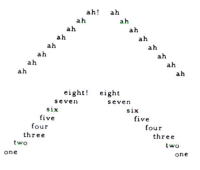

2. *Singing and Speaking through an Octave on a Number
Sequence.*

    a. Sing "One" on the same starting note as in Exercise 1.
Start to sing it again, but change over to speech by
sliding up in pitch from where you started and then
cutting the syllable off short. You will find that you
change to speech as soon as you begin the upward
slide. Continue with the number sequence up the
octave, singing the first of each pair, sliding into
speech with the second. The speaking of each number
should begin exactly on the pitch at which it was
sung.

    Numbers underlined below are to be sung, the others
spoken. The exclamation point suggests the rising
pitch of the spoken number. "Eight" only is spoken
with a falling inflection.

```
                                             eight, ei
                                                      ght
                                    seven,  seven!
                           six,  six!
                      five,  five!
                 four,  four!
            three,  three!
       two,  two!
  one,  one!
```

b. Repeat *a*, singing down the scale, and using a falling
inflection on each spoken number except "One,"
which is spoken at a level low pitch.

```
                                             eight, ei
                                                      ght
                                    seven,  sev
                                                en
                           six,  si
                                    x
                      five,  fi
                               ve
                 four,  fo
                           ur
            three,  thr
                         ee
       two,  tw
                o
  one,  one
```

3. *Singing and Speaking a Rapid, Rhythmic Number
Sequence.* In the following exercise first sing the number
sequence rapidly up and down single intervals of the octave.
The first and the fifth number of each group is accented as
shown by underlining. Then speak the sequence with the same
rhythm and with a rising and falling inflection pattern which
corresponds with the pattern of the melody of the sung
sequence. Speak as rapidly and smoothly as you sang.

Repeat the exercise, starting the first repetition one note
higher for the sung sequence and slightly higher in pitch for
the spoken sequence. With further repetitions, move the starting
note now higher, now lower by single intervals until strain is
felt. Daily, as you do the exercise, work for higher and lower
levels of sung and spoken pitch.

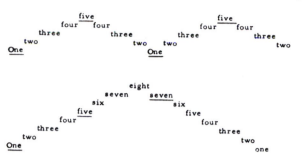

4. *Sliding in Speech Pitch on Vowels and Diphthongs.* Precede this exercise with a wide yawn and a deep inhalation. Speak each of the seven syllables below on a long, continuous pitch slide, beginning at your lowest speech pitch, sliding up gradually and steadily to your highest. Reverse the process, sliding all the way down on the eighth syllable.

Note that the series begins with vowels which are made at the back of the mouth and are basically low in pitch and ends with high front vowels naturally high in pitch.

As you become familiar with the exercise, widen your pitch range day by day until you can span two octaves in one slide.

Mah, maw, moh, moo, mow, my, may, me

To vary it, slide freely up or down on any syllable in the series.

GROUP C. USING PITCH VARIATIONS IN SPEAKING AND READING

1. *Speaking with Pitch Leaps and Slides.* Speak the following phrases and sentences, using leaps in pitch up or down as suggested by the spacing. Vary the readings by using speech slides of your own invention.

```
Down,                    well!    Oh

    down,              well,

      down.   Well,                no!
```

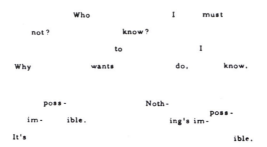

2. *Practicing Speech Builds.* Speak, answering a second actor as shown below. Let the pitch rise or fall sharply.

On the build below, alternate, beginning with the lowest-pitched words, each topping the other, till your highest possible pitch is reached.

3. *Responding to Content with Varying Pitches.* Study the following poems to absorb their content and style. Immerse yourself in the mood of each, tragic and violent respectively. Then present each as if it were a monologue from a play. Allow pitch change to happen according to the emotions the poems quicken.

From ELEGY: FOR TWENTY-THREE YOUNG GIRLS
DROWNED OFF THE ISLAND OF CRETE, 1972

" . . . desires fell mutely on the waves and drowned
like lovesick girls for whom the world seems too confined."
NIKOS KAZANTZAKIS (tr. KIMON FRIAR)

1. The Day

The day began like a casual mistake . . .
The day overturned with the small skiff overloaded with children . . .
The children drowned . . .

2. The Girl

I am wise now: I have no desires.

I have become like the water,
a continual sound to others,
who have desires.

But I wanted once so many things:
the boys at school
to see I no longer moved like a child,
the baker not to pinch me so
when I went to his shop for tsoureki,   tsoo-ré-kee
I wanted to brush and brush my hair
with a violent tenderness
and an understanding between us.
I wanted to watch my breasts grow full and firm
like the breasts of my sister,
the dark centers yearning for something.
I wanted my eyes to startle,
and to hide their alarm, like a woman's.
So many things.
I wanted to lie down—not in the sea—
and feel the turning of grass in the wind
like a light hand over all my body,
moving slowly slowly down my slimness
to the new curve of my hips.
I wanted a lover . . .

. . . I wanted to learn.
I wanted my own despair.

GARY MIRANDA

GOING HOME

Going home
see had me a thing with a cop.
after walking my girl home they picked me up
on the street. where you going this hour of night?

been walking my girl.
where she live?
a long way from here.
what bus you take?

why you asking me these questions
then he jumps from his car
you getting smart with me son?
no sir   I could smell his toughness

Where you been?
My girl's

you better stop lying. he looks at the other cop.
this boy thinks he's smart or something
then he starts to feel my behind
and then I jump as I always do when someone feels my behind
oh shit, he says when I jumps, did you see that?
that boy was going to hit me   then he hit me.

run he said so I saw now
how it was going to be for me that night
boy, if you run i going to blow your head off   run he said
he kicked me pushed me with his gun then when he saw
i was not going to run he put away his gun   *then* i run

me running smelling the streets bumping into dark gates.

TURK, in *Young Voices from the Black Ghetto*

4. *Using Varying Pitch to Express Sophistication.* "O
Cheese" may be read individually or as a group exercise, each
describing his favorite cheese with enthusiasm.

O CHEESE

In the pantry the dear dense cheeses, Cheddars and harsh
Lancashires; Gorgonzola with its magnanimous manner;
the clipped speech of Roquefort; and a head of Stilton
that speaks in a sensuous riddling tongue like Druids.

O cheeses of gravity, cheeses of wistfulness, cheeses
that weep continually because they know they will die.
O cheeses of victory, cheeses wise in defeat, cheeses
fat as a cushion, lolling in bed until noon.

Liederkranz ebullient, jumping like a small dog, noisy;
Pont l'Evêque intellectual, and quite well informed; Emmentaler
decent and loyal, a little deaf in the right ear;
and Brie the revealing experience, instantaneous and profound.

O cheeses that dance in the moonlight, cheeses
that mingle with sausages, cheeses of Stonehenge.
O cheeses that are shy, that linger in the doorway,
eyes looking down, cheeses spectacular as fireworks.

Reblochon openly sexual; Caerphilly like pine trees, small
at the timberline; Port du Salut in love; Caprice des Dieux
eloquent, tactful, like a thousand-year-old hostess;
and Dolcelatte, always generous to a fault.

O village of cheeses, I make you this poem of cheeses,
O family of cheeses, living together in pantries,
O cheeses that keep to your own nature, like a lucky couple,
this solitude, this energy, these bodies slowly dying.

DONALD HALL

5. Exaggerate your pitch changes for the following. See also
the limericks on pages 123-25.

> There was a young man who cried "Damn!
> At last I perceive what I am!
>   A creature that moves
>   In predestinate grooves—
> Not a bus, not a bus, but a tram!"

ANONYMOUS

> There's a notable family called Stein,
> There's Gertrude, there's Ep, and there's Ein.
>   Gert's poems are punk.
>   Ep's statues are junk,
> And I can't make a thing out of Ein.

ANONYMOUS

6. More exercises in pitch variation appear in Appendix C.

GROUP D. EXERCISES FOR VARIETY OF SPEED

1. Read the speeches below fluently and fast.

ALGERNON: I haven't the smallest intention of doing anything of the kind. To begin with, I dined there on Monday, and once a week is quite enough to dine with one's own relatives. In the second place, whenever I do dine there, I am always treated as a member of the family, and sent down with either no woman at all, or two. In the third place I know perfectly well whom she will place me next to tonight. She will place me next to Mary Farquhar, who always flirts with her own husband across the dinnertable. That is not very pleasant. Indeed, it is not even decent . . . and that sort of thing is enormously on the increase. The amount of women in London who flirt with their own husbands is perfectly scandalous. It looks so bad. It is simply washing one's clean linen in public. Besides, now that I know you to be a confirmed Bunburyist I naturally want to talk to you about Bunburying. I want to tell you the rules.

LADY BRACKNELL: Well, I must say, Algernon, that I think it is high time that Mr. Bunbury made up his mind whether he is going to live or die. This shilly-shallying with the question is absurd. Nor do I in any way approve of the modern sympathy with invalids. I consider it morbid. Illness of any kind is hardly a thing to be encouraged in others. Health is the primary duty of life. I am always telling that to your poor uncle, but he never seems to take much notice . . . as far as any improvement in his ailments goes. I should be much obliged if you would ask Mr. Bunbury, from me, to be kind enough not to have a relapse on Saturday, for I rely on you to arrange my music for me. It is my last reception and one wants something that will encourage conversation, particularly at the end of the season when everyone has practically said whatever they had to say, which, in most cases, was probably not much.

OSCAR WILDE, *The Importance of Being Earnest*

2. Read the selections below with varying speeds, appropriate to the content.

(1)

I only know that you may lie
Daylong, and watch the Cambridge sky,
And flower-lulled in sleepy grass
Hear the cool lapse of hours pass,

Until the centuries blend and blur
In Grantchester, in Grantchester.
RUPERT BROOKE, The Old Vicarage, Grantchester

(2)

INVERSNAID

This darksome burn, horseback brown,
His rollrock highroad roaring down,
In coop and in comb the fleece of his foam
Flutes and low to the lake falls home.

A windpuff bonnet of fawn-froth
Turns and twindles over the broth
Of a pool so pitchblack, fell-frowning
It rounds and rounds Despair to drowning.

Dogged with dew, dappled with dew
Are the groins of the braes that the brook treads through,
Wiry heathpacks, flitches of fern,
And the beadbonny ash that sits over the burn.

What would the world be, once bereft
Of wet and of wildness? Let them be left,
O let them be left, wildness and wet;
Long live the weeds and the wilderness yet.
GERARD MANLÉY HOPKINS

(3) The selection from Walt Whitman, in Chapter 6.
(4) The selections from the Exercises for the Correction of Stridency, in the Appendix.
(5) The following scene from *Antony and Cleopatra:*

ANTONY: I am dying, Egypt, dying; only
I here importune death awhile, until
Of many thousand kisses the poor last
I lay upon thy lips. . .
                    O quick! or I am gone.

CLEOPATRA: Here's sport indeed! How heavy weighs my lord!
Our strength is all gone into heaviness,
That makes the weight. Had I great Juno's power
The strong-winged Mercury should fetch thee up,

And set thee by Jove's side. Yet come a little,
Wishers were ever fools. O! come, come, come;
They heave Antony aloft to Cleopatra.

And welcome, welcome! die where thou hast lived;
Quicken with kissing; had my lips that power
Thus would I wear them out. . .

ANTONY: I am dying, Egypt, dying;
Give me some wine, and let me speak a little . . .
The miserable change now at my end
Lament nor sorrow at, but please your thoughts
In feeding them with those my former fortunes
Wherein I lived, the greatest prince o' the world,
The noblest; and do now not basely die,
Not cowardly put off my helmet to
My countryman; a Roman by a Roman
Valiantly vanquished. Now my spirit is going;
I can no more.

CLEOPATRA: Noblest of men, woo't die?
Hast thou no care of me? shall I abide
In this dull world, which in thy absence is
No better than a sty? O see, my women,

Antony dies.

The crown o' the earth doth melt. My lord!
O withered is the garland of the war,
The soldier's pole is fallen; young boys and girls
Are level now with men; the odds is gone,
And there is nothing left remarkable
Beneath the visiting moon.

(6) Read scenes from plays of your choice in which
slow speaking speed is sometimes appropriate.

GROUP E. EXERCISES FOR DEVELOPING VARIETY OF
SPEECH STRESS

Directions: Do exercises 1 through 9 from the Actor's Warm-
Up Series in preparation.

1. *Practicing Stress Variations on Single Words*
   a. Repeat each of the following words five times, with slowly increasing stress. Allow the pitch to rise a little.

   Yes.　No.　You?　Why?　Mine.

   b. First whisper the following words, then utter them with great stress:

   Now.　Never.　Go.　Hush.　Do!

   c. Count-Down. Count as if at a rocket firing, with slightly increasing stress:

Ten, nine, eight, seven, six, five, four, three, two, one, zero!

2. *Practicing Contrasting Stress.* Contrast in pitch and stress when there is an instant transition from high pitch and strong stress to low pitch and restrained stress, may be an effective theatrical device. Experiment with the following, using rising pitch and stress with the first sequence, dropping sharply to the opposite with the monosyllabic reply:

   Yes, yes, yes!—No.
   No, no, no!—Yes.
   Hurry, hurry, hurry!—Wait.
   Why, why, why?—Why not?
   Who did it, who did it, who did it?—I did.

3. *Practicing Single Stresses.* Stress only one word in each of the following quotations. Observe how the meaning is affected by your choice of a word. Raise the pitch appropriately on the stressed word.

I washed my face and hands afore I come, I did.
GEORGE BERNARD SHAW, *Pygmalion*

Well, it's a terror to be aged a score.
JOHN SYNGE, *Playboy of the Western World*

A father,—a father for the Superman!
GEORGE BERNARD SHAW, *Man and Superman*

I'll have her dog destroyed.
RUDOLF BESIER, *The Barretts of Wimpole Street*

It's what every woman knows, John.
J. M. BARRIE, *What Every Woman Knows*

I think to him they were all my sons. And I guess they were.
I guess they were.
ARTHUR MILLER, *All My Sons*

You must wear your rue with a difference.
SHAKESPEARE, *Hamlet*

I'm in mourning for my life.
ANTON CHEKHOV, *The Seagull*
(tr. by Elizabeth Fen)

Maggie, I didn't dare ask you: my books! They haven't been
lost, have they?
THORNTON WILDER, *The
Skin of Our Teeth*

I'm burning your child, Thea. Burning it, curly-locks.
HENRIK IBSEN, *Hedda Gabler*

The valiant never taste of death but once.
SHAKESPEARE, *Julius Caesar*

Who's afraid of Virginia Woolf . . .
I . . . am . . . George . . . I . . . am! . . .
EDWARD ALBEE, *Who's Afraid of Virginia Woolf?*

4. *Reading Aloud with Varying Stresses*

    a. In Hopkins' poem below, the stresses and rhythms tend to be more like those of vigorous speech than metrical poetry. Read the poem aloud, first accenting the italicized words, guiding the stress of the voice against the pull of the meter. Read it again with other accented words chosen by yourself.

GOD'S GRANDEUR

The world is charged with the grandeur of God.
    It will *flame* out, like shining from shook foil;
    It gathers to a greatness, like the ooze of oil
Crushed. Why do men then now *not reck* his rod?
Generations have trod, have trod, have trod,
    And all is *seared* with trade; bleared, *smeared* with toil;
    And wears man's *smudge* and shares man's *smell:* the soil
Is bare now, nor can foot *feel,* being shod.

And for all this, nature is *never* spent;
    There lives the dearest freshness *deep down* things;
And though the last lights off the black West went
    Oh, morning, at the brown brink eastward, *springs*
Because the Holy Ghost over the bent
    World *broods* with *warm* breast and with *ah! bright* wings.
                         GERARD MANLEY HOPKINS

    b. In Shakespeare's Sonnet CXXXV below, the italics are his. Read the poem aloud, stressing the italicized words, and any others needed to bring out the double meanings.

Whoever hath her wish, thou hast thy *Will,*
And *Will* to boot, and *Will* in over-plus;
More than enough am I that vex thee still,
To thy sweet will making addition thus.
Wilt thou, whose will is large and spacious,
Not once vouchsafe to hide my will in thine?
Shall will in others seem right gracious,
And in my will no fair acceptance shine?
The sea, all water, yet receives rain still,
And in abundance addeth to his store;

So thou, being rich in *Will*, add to thy *Will*
One will of mine, to make thy large *Will* more.
Let no unkind 'No' fair beseechers kill;
Think all but one, and me in that one *Will*.

5. Work on scenes demanding intense stress in speech, violent or restrained. You may find them in Lillian Hellman's *The Little Foxes,* Edward Albee's *Who's Afraid of Virginia Woolf?,* David Storey's *Home,* Howard Sackler's *The Great White Hope,* Peter Shaffer's *Equus,* and others.

6. Read the following with the harsh stress called for. (All male black South Africans must go to a pass office to get their Registration Certificates, where they wait in queues for hours, sometimes days, to be attended to.)

PASS OFFICE SONG

Take off your hat.
What is your home name?
Who is your father?
Who is your chief?
Where do you pay your tax?
What river do you drink?

We mourn for our country.

PEGGY RUTHERFORD, trans.

7. More exercises for variety appear in Appendix C.

10 | ⁓

The Speaking
of Shakespeare

> ...Use all gently: for in the very torrent,
> tempest, and, as I may say, whirlwind of pas-
> sion, you must acquire and beget a temper-
> ance that may give it smoothness.
>
> *Hamlet to the Players*

THE ABILITY TO speak Shakespeare's lines well is a near
necessity to a contemporary versatile actor. Recent years
have seen a tremendous revival of interest in Shakespeare
and his contemporaries in England, in Canada, and in
the United States.

Restoration plays also made a comeback in all three
countries, with brilliant productions such as *The School
for Scandal, The Recruiting Sergeant,* and many others.
Medieval verse dramas too began to be revived with great
success. *The Play of Daniel* in the United States and E.
Martin Browne's productions of religious drama such as the
Coventry Cycle, presented lately in the ruins of Coventry
Cathedral aroused wide interest.

Shakespeare, however, has had the strongest impact on
modern theatre. After World War I and through the
early 1930s, his plays were produced in a fairly traditional
manner in the (then) new Memorial Theatre at Stratford
upon Avon. During these years, English touring compa-
nies brought similar productions to Canada and the United

States. Early in the 1950s came a revolution in the performance of Shakespeare at England's Stratford and the sudden, meteoric rise of the Canadian Stratford Festival in Ontario, with productions so lively in conception and magnificent in execution that it won international recognition in a few years. There followed the organization of the American Stratford Festival in Connecticut, slowly evolving toward a permanent repertory company that in the 1960s was to challenge the Canadian theatre for first place. In the 1950s, also, Joseph Papp conceived and brought into being his Shakespeare in Central Park, New York—free, open-air productions that attracted capacity audiences. During the same period other community and university festivals came into being throughout the United States and Canada, making a continentwide revival. Shakespeare's quatercentenary saw a burst of notable productions all over the English-speaking world.

Then and now there are increasing opportunities in Shakespearean roles for the actor sufficiently trained in both movement and speech to take advantage of them. Prepare yourself for such opportunities by developing your speech to a high point of excellence, and, as equally important, undertaking training in dance and in fencing.

You must also know your Shakespeare. Begin by seeing and hearing his plays. You are fortunate if you meet them first on the stage rather than in the classroom. The plays were meant to be experienced through the ear and the eye, not through the printed page. Therefore, go to every performance you can possibly attend. The good productions will teach you why Shakespeare has survived for three hundred years and will for a thousand more. Even poor productions are much nearer the real Shakespeare than are the collected works. But fine performances are your best possible teachers. Try to see a good production two or three times during its run. Much detail that you would otherwise miss will then impress itself upon your memory. Both your eye and ear will be educated as you watch the pageantry of the action and hear the sweep of the language, ranging from magnificence to vulgarity.

Even if you cannot often attend Shakespeare's plays, you can and should listen to them often. Collect a library of the best recorded productions available, as suggested in Chapter 1. Hear a play over and over, straight through, without the text in your hand. Enjoy it as one enjoys a symphony, getting to know it as a whole and discovering for yourself its most poetic, most humorous, or most ironic passages. Then listen to its great speeches. If some of the passages are obscure, you will find that simply to hear them well spoken makes their meanings clearer. You will be saved from the kind of lamentable ignorance displayed by one young actor Joseph Papp tells of. Auditioning for the part of the Chorus in *Henry V*, he thought he saw an opportunity approaching for a rousing cry and gave it his all:

> Can we cram
> Within this wooden,—*OH!* the very casques
> That did affright the air at Agincourt?

Had he seen or heard it spoken on the stage as a description of Shakespeare's Globe, he would have read it correctly:

> Can we cram
> Within *this wooden O* the very casques
> That did affright the air at Agincourt?

Pitch transcription may be used, as described in the last chapter, for analyzing some of the notable lines. You may compare one recorded reading with others and realize how infinite in faculty is man the actor. Copy several readings successively onto one tape, and find out how differently a Burton, a Scofield, an Olivier, a Redgrave, or a Gielgud reads such lines as

> I'll call thee Hamlet,
> King, father,—royal Dane, O answer me!

Act in a Shakespeare play whenever you get the chance. Even if you must be content with a small role, resolve to learn all that you can through listening to your fellow-actors struggling with the difficulties of blank verse and Elizabethan idiom. Hearing whole acts and scenes repeatedly will impress them on your memory. You will then think of them as acting sequences, not as numbered lines on a page. As the text of a play becomes familiar to you and as you act out your own role, you will feel the relationship of the parts to the whole throughout the play.

Supplement this threefold ear-training with study to clear up any difficulties you meet. Use a good set of notes, like those in the Kittredge *Shakespeare*, and a complete glossary, like Oliver T. Onions' *A Shakespeare Glossary*, published by the Oxford University Press. This study is best done when needed. You can hardly speak a puzzling line like

> If a man were porter of Hellgate, he should have *old* turning the
> key,

without first looking up the idiom and discovering that *old* here means *plenty of*. Emphasizing it will then bring out the meaning.

The study of Shakespeare in your literature classes, if linked with acting opportunities, may be a most enriching experience. All the background books that you can read, particularly original sources like the diary of Philip Henslowe, who managed the rival company to Shakespeare's, or Hakluyt's *Voyages*, or Holinshed's *Chronicles*, will make your grasp of the plays and the people in them more complete.

To actually speak the lines, you will need to master each of the separate speech techniques described in this book, relaxation, breath control, resonance, articulation, and variety. As to breath control, for example, Tyrone Guthrie declares that a Shakespearean actor should be able to speak a whole sonnet on one breath only! Such an accomplishment hardly makes for good interpretation of the sonnet, since one must speak at top speed throughout to manage it. But the economical use of breath required, not a cubic centimeter of it wasted, is a fine preparation for reading the long speeches which are scattered throughout the plays. The ghost in *Hamlet*, for example, has a speech of forty-five unbroken lines. The King in *Henry V* speaks for fifty-five lines at once (IV, i). And Richard II, in the prison scene, continues uninterrupted for sixty-six lines!

Often these speeches should be spoken rapidly, in groups of lines with but one breath to a group. Otherwise, they might seem unbearably long. It is obvious that your breath control for such speeches will have to be highly efficient.

The breaking up of long speeches into units, one breath to a unit, also keeps them from getting dull. Long exposition speeches are especially helped by this technique. If, for instance, you are playing the Archbishop of Canterbury in *Henry V*, you must handle much of the text which explains to the audience that the young prince is a reformed character since his father's death. Keep this exposition going by speeding along on as few breaths as possible, taking them perhaps only at the diagonals shown below:

> The breath no sooner left his father's body
> But that his wildness, mortified in him,
> Seem'd to die too;/yea, at that very moment
> Consideration like an angel came

And whipp'd the offending Adam out of him,
Leaving his body as a Paradise
To envelop and contain celestial spirits./
Never was such a sudden scholar made;/
Never came reformation in a flood
With such a heady currance, scouring faults;/
Nor never Hydra-headed wilfulness
So soon did lose his seat and all at once
As in this king./

Henry V, I, i

Your tone, like your breath control, must be strongly developed. Refresh your resonance techniques frequently, returning to the exercises of Chapter 7 for this purpose. The more musical your tone is, the finer will be the sound of the poetry. It is the same Archbishop quoted above who says of the prince,

Hear his discourse of war, and you shall hear
A fearful battle rendered you *in music*.

Remember this comment if, as Hotspur, you must describe the rough action of the single combat between Mortimer and Glendower (*Henry IV*, Part I, I, iii.) Remember it at the other extreme, when Shakespeare lets the whole action of the play pause for the enjoyment of poetry, and the flight of soaring images. Give your fullest resonance as well as your strongest sense of delight and wonder to lines like those describing bees as

The singing masons building roofs of gold,

or flowers as courageous:

Daffodils
That come before the swallow dares, and take
The winds of March with beauty:

or twilight as coming like water streaming into a great bowl:

> The pouring dark
> Fills the wide vessel of the universe.

A musical speaking voice was easy for Elizabethan actors to achieve. The boy-actresses of Shakespeare's company were often recruited from the Cathedral choir schools, where they had had long training in singing and chanting, which must have benefited their speech.

The men in Shakespeare's company, too, must have had good singing voices. Music in the Elizabethan age was a part of every educated man and woman's life. Had you lived then, you would have been able to pick up a madrigal or motet, and sing any part suitable for your voice at sight. Singing

> With wanton heed, and giddy cunning,
> The melting voice in mazes running;

is one of the common joys Milton describes in "L'Allegro." Actors could sing then, since everyone sang for pleasure, not as a performer. It will be greatly to your advantage if you too sing for pleasure and like the Elizabethans carry the music of singing tone into your speech.

Your articulation must be flawless. The main problem with amateur and with some professional Shakespeare productions is that the actors do not make the words understood. This points to a general slovenliness of articulation, since many of the most famous lines are made up of one syllable words, which only need to be spoken very simply and clearly. Surprisingly, they often occur at the height of the action. Thus, Lear with the dead Cordelia:

> Howl, howl, howl, howl!—O, you are men of stones:
> Had I your tongues and eyes, I'd use them so
> That heaven's vault should crack.—She's gone for ever!
> I know when one is dead and when one lives;
> She's dead as earth . . .
> No, no, no life!

> Why should a dog, a horse, a rat have life,
> And thou no breath at all? Thou'lt come no more . . .

or Othello, nerving himself to strangle Desdemona:

> It is the cause, it is the cause, my soul!
> Let me not name it to you, you chaste stars!
> It is the cause.—Yet I'll not shed her blood,
> Nor scar that whiter skin of hers than snow . . .

or Prince Arthur, in *King John,* imploring Hubert not to blind him.

> Let me not hold my tongue,—let me not, Hubert!
> Or Hubert, if you will, cut out my tongue
> So I may keep my eyes,—O, spare my eyes,
> Though to no use but still to look on you!

or Romeo, gazing at Juliet on her balcony:

> See how she leans her cheek upon her hand!
> O that I were a glove upon that hand
> That I might touch that cheek!

or Hamlet, in an agony of indecision:

>   I do not know
> Why yet I live to say *This thing's to do,*
> Sith I have cause, and will, and strength, and means
> To do it.

Many more examples could be given. And if the lines with words of no more than one or two syllables were to be counted, they would comprise the great bulk of the plays. This is not the learned language of a scholar. It is the language of the common man, dramatic because it is direct. You should perfect your articulation so that these lines have an immediate, powerful impact on the hearer.

You must take additional care with instances of more complex articulation. Some lines repeatedly use awkward consonant combinations. When you meet these, apply to them the lip-whisper-speak sequence as described in Chapter 8 under Exercises for Agility of Articulation. By this means you may achieve absolute precision, even with repeated *st*'s as in

> Let me not name it to you, you chaste stars!

"You chase stars" is to be avoided at all costs. Other consonant groups that are troublesome are *dst*'s, as in the repeated "wouldst" spoken by Lady Macbeth. The actress must keep her lips rounded for the *w* while she makes the triple tongue movement for *dst*:

> Thou *wouldst* be great,
> Art not without ambition, but without
> The illness should attend it; what thou *wouldst* highly
> That thou *wouldst* holily; *wouldst* not play false,
> And yet *wouldst* wrongly win.

Another sound often lax in American speech is the tongue-tip consonant *l*. The many *l*'s in Polonius' speech below need to be firmly made, tongue pressing upwards on the gum-ridge:

> The best actors in the world, either for tragedy, comedy, history, pastoral, pastoral-comical, historical-pastoral, tragical-historical, tragical-comical-historical-pastoral, scene individable or poem unlimited.

Closely related to articulation difficulties is the communication of the archaic word or obsolete idiom as in the examples below. When these occur, they may puzzle the listener. Do not cover them up by slurring them. Rather, articulate them very clearly, so that your hearer may know what he heard, strange though it sounds. Emphasize them, in fact, and let context, inflection, and business bring out their meanings:

>   . . . spies and speculations
> Intelligent of our state; what hath been seen
> Either in *snuffs* or *packings* of the dukes
> Or the hard rein which both have often borne
> Against the old kind king.
>
>   *King Lear*

>   When I dissuaded him from his intent
> And found him *pight* to do it, with curst speech
> I threatened to discover him.
>
>   *King Lear*

> How will this *fadge?* My master loves her dearly,
> And I, poor monster, *fond* as much on him.
>
>   *Twelfth Night*

Supplement good tone and good articulation with variety in your speech. Of the three techniques of variety, stress is perhaps the most important in the speaking of Shakespeare. Stressing the right words, and the right words only, makes the meanings clear. Margaret Webster calls this the "telegram" approach. She tells her actors that Shakespeare means what he says and says what he means, and nothing else! Therefore, she suggests imagining that you are going to send a speech as a telegram by reducing it to the fewest possible words. These are the words to stress. They will lift the meaning right out of the context and focus the attention of the audience on it. Typical telegram words might be those in italics in Angelo's soliloquy:

> What's this? what's this? Is this *her* fault *or mine?*
> Ha!
> The *tempter* or the *tempted*, who sins most?
> *Not she;* nor doth she tempt; but it is *I*
> That, lying by the violet, in the sun
> Do, as the carrion does, not as the flower,
> *Corrupt* with virtuous season. *Can* it be
> That *modesty* may *more* betray our sense
> Than woman's *lightness?* Having waste ground enough,
> Shall we desire to *raze* the *sanctuary*
> And pitch our evils *there?* O, fie, fie, fie!
> What *dost* thou? or what *art* thou, Angelo?

Dost thou desire her *foully* for those things
That make her *good?* O, let her *brother live;*
Measure for Measure, II, ii

Careful choice of stressed words may also help to
avoid overemphasizing the meter. The lines are all in
iambic pentameter, but you must not accent each beat
even when the verse is regular. Otherwise, the effect will
be a singsong evenness:

Your hands than mine are quicker for a fray,
My legs are longer, though, to run away.

A Midsummer Night's Dream

Rather, stress the telegram words:

Your hands than mine are *quicker* for a fray,
My legs are *longer,* though, to run *away.*

This overcomes the worst of the monotony. With any lines
that are not end-stopped, the meaning continuing into
the next line, you may disrupt the beat by reading straight
on, moving the pause from the end of the line to where
the sense pauses next. This makes the lines sound like
natural conversation:

LORENZO: Sit, Jessica. Look how the floor of heaven is thick inlaid
with patines of bright gold! There's not the smallest orb that
thou behold'st but in his motion like an angel sings, still quiring
to the young-eyed cherubims. Such harmony is in immortal souls;
but whilst this muddy vesture of decay doth grossly close it in,
we cannot hear it.

The Merchant of Venice

The same moving of the pause away from the end of the
line makes even a solemn intercession sound like a natural
prayer:

KING: O God of battles, steel my soldiers' hearts!
Possess them not with fear, Take from them now
the sense of reckoning, if the opposed numbers
pluck their hearts from them. Not to-day, O
Lord, O, not to-day, think not upon the fault my
father made in compassing the crown!

Henry V

In a production of *Romeo and Juliet* at the Canadian Stratford Festival, there was an interesting solution to the problem of how to read the stiffly regular lines which are spoken by the lovers at their first meeting. These actually comprise a perfect sonnet. The director, Tyrone Guthrie, made a virtue of necessity, creating from the static quality of the sonnet a memorable moment of theatre. The Capulets' ball was proceeding with a dance of rotating couples which brought Romeo and Juliet downstage center on the last line preceding the sonnet. At that moment the motion of the dance stopped, the music diminished, and the dancers remained fixed in whatever attitudes they had just assumed. The lights dimmed, except on Romeo and Juliet, where they brightened. Both the dreamlike sense of suspended animation and the concentration of light on the pair heightened the intensity of the moment and caught the attention of the audience. The sonnet was spoken gravely and rhythmically, each lover answering quatrain with quatrain, couplet with couplet, and line with line, with the simplest of readings. The first and second kiss were given and taken as in a moment of enchantment. Then the Nurse intruded, calling Juliet away. With her voice, the spell snapped, the dance was resumed, and the lovers were parted.

Speed is also an important element of variety in Shakespearean speech. It may be increased or decreased according to the pace of the dramatic action. Heroic characters and humorous characters alike may speak very rapidly. Shakespeare's low-life characters, and their high-born associates, too, usually speak in prose, which runs along at a swift pace. Falstaff, in *The Merry Wives of Windsor*, lightly commiserates on his plight; the actor must not make heavy weather of it but must keep it easy and quick:

> Have I lived to be carried in a basket, like a barrow
> of butcher's offal; and to be thrown into the Thames?
> Well, if I ever be served such another trick, I'll have
> my brains ta'en out and butter'd, and give them to a dog
> for a new year's gift. The rogues slighted me
> into the river with as little remorse as they would have
> drowned a bitch's blind puppies, fifteen i' the litter;
> and you may know by my size that I have a kind of
> alacrity in sinking; if the bottom were deep as hell I
> should down.

Speed is even more important at a moment of danger, as in the first scene of *The Tempest*. There is a shouted fury of haste in the Boatswain's speeches. There must be mechanical precision of articulation along with the high speed, however, or the audience will not catch the words:

> Down with the top-mast; yare; lower, lower; bring her
> to try with the main-course. . . . Lay her a-hold, a-
> hold; set her two courses; off to sea again, lay
> her off!

Slow speed in speaking has the opposite effect. It may help an actor to play a restrained, deliberate character, one who makes his decision from reason, not from passion. You may hear such speech by listening to Laurence Olivier as Othello on the record *Homage to Shakespeare*. He meets the rage of Desdemona's father with a calm, slow-paced statement of how Desdemona came to marry him:

> She loved me for the dangers I had passed,
> And I loved her that she did pity them.
> This only is the witch-craft I have us'd.

Finally, your use of pitch change and pitch range for Shakespearean speech will relate to every other speech technique you use. Pitch change may strengthen the frequencies of certain vowels as the inflection rises or falls. Articulation at high speed usually requires high pitch, as does increased stress. Accordingly, apply all three in situations where you must keep the scene moving, even though the lines are composed of a long list of items, usually words or phrases in apposition. Hamlet itemizes in one of his soliloquies:

> For who would bear the whips and scorns of time,
> The oppressor's wrong, the proud man's contumely,
> The pangs of despis'd love, the law's delay,
> The insolence of office, and the spurns
> That patient merit of the unworthy takes . . .

Malcolm has a list of adjectives to describe Macbeth:

> I grant him bloody,
> Luxurious, avaricious, false, deceitful,
> Sudden, malicious, smacking of every sin
> That has a name . . .

and of himself he says:

> The king-becoming graces
> Are justice, verity, temperance, stableness,
> Bounty, perseverance, mercy, lowliness,
> Devotion, patience, courage, fortitude,—
> I have no relish of them.

In speaking such a list, let your pitch rise very gradually, so that the last item on the list may have the highest pitch and the greatest intensity. Or you may move through changing levels from high to low pitch and back again. Some element of varying pitch you must use; otherwise, you will achieve only monotonous reiteration.

In working on a long speech, you should usually try

to find in it a series of lesser climaxes leading up to the main one. Think of it as a mountain range which must be crossed. First climb the lower foothills, then the lesser heights, with valleys between. Finally scale the highest peak, reaching the great climax of the speech, when you may truly be crying out "on top of the question." Either the speech ends abruptly at such a point,

> Cry, God for Harry, England and Saint George!
>
> *Henry V*

or there may be a gradual descent, varied with occasional uprushes of energy, until the plain of quiet utterance is reached again:

> This music mads me; let it sound no more;
> For though it have holp madmen to their wits,
> In me it seems it will make wise men mad.
> Yet blessing on his heart that gives it me!
> For 'tis a sign of love; and love to Richard
> Is a strange brooch in this all-hating world.
>
> *Richard II*

The problems involved in learning to speak Shakespeare's lines are many and complex. You should not expect to master them in a hurry. You will presently reach the point where speech techniques begin to fuse with acting techniques, for it is impossible to speak the speech as the spirit of Shakespeare pronounces it to you and not find yourself acting the part. Accordingly, allow yourself plenty of time. Follow the program outlined below, which may take you a year or two to complete. It offers twenty-four scenes each for a man or a woman as the main character. They are arranged in order of slowly increasing difficulty. In a year's program, you may work on each for two or more weeks and then deliver it before an audience as suggested.

Meanwhile, continue your ear-training, making every effort to attend the great festivals at the three Stratfords and to see the British National Theatre and the Royal Shakespeare Theatre when these are on tour. As your own repertoire grows, your ear will respond with delight when a passage you know is spoken magnificently on the stage, every syllable clear, every meaning scored. The reverse is true, too. Dull readings, careless articulation, and weak projection will madden you.

But far more pleasure than pain awaits you. Train your ear both to accept the good and to reject the bad, until your standards are of the highest. Ultimately you too may play your part, not "as an unperfect actor on the stage," but as one able to fulfil

> . . . the purpose of playing, whose end, both at the first and now, was, and is, to hold, as 'twere, the mirror up to nature.
>
> *Hamlet*

Listening to Records of Shakespeare's Plays

For one year, listen once a month to one of the recorded plays of Shakespeare or selected speeches from Shakespeare, from the records listed in The Actor's Listening Library. Note which scenes give you the most theatrical kind of experience.

Exercises in Preparing Scenes from Shakespeare

The scenes listed below offer a sequence from the comedies, histories, and tragedies of Shakespeare for the actor or actress. In preparing them for performance, follow the steps as outlined, working with fellow-actors as needed, with a director if possible.

1. *Studying the Scene in Relation to the Play*. Each scene has one or more main characters, with or without minor sup-

porting roles. The scene is a highlight of its particular play, and the main character is at a moment of importance theatrically. Assume a main character part yourself. Read first the scene itself, then the act from which it came, then the entire play. Listen to it as recorded by a good company. Then begin to work, spending at least two weeks on it before performance.

2. *Preparing to Speak the Scene.* Attack the speech first by roughly planning out the breath pauses while you are memorizing the lines. Always practice them with fully resonant tone. Iron out articulation problems by the lip-whisper-say technique. Find inflections by letting the situation of the character and the mood of the scene take hold of your imagination and guide your readings. Throw away stiffness by paraphrasing the lines into modern speech, as in the following example:

> Kneel not, gentle Portia.
>
> I should not need, if you were gentle Brutus.
> Within the bond of marriage, tell me, Brutus,
> Is it excepted I should know no secrets
> That appertain to you?
>
> Julius Caesar
>
> Dear Portia, don't kneel!
>
> If you were dear Brutus, I shouldn't have to. We're married, and don't you think a wife ought to share her husband's secrets, some of them, anyway?

Carry the natural vivid inflections you used in the paraphrase back into the lines as Shakespeare wrote them. When they seem easy and familiar as you speak them, tape-record your reading and judge if it is clear and comprehensible.

3. *Preparing the Movement for the Scene.* Decide whether the prevailing mood of the scene is one of energy, calmness, or exaltation. If it is energy, whether of gaiety, impatience, haste, or danger, it will require action. When you move in such a scene, do so freely, vigorously, and with intent, as Martha

Graham would say. If the mood is one of calmness, you may scarcely move at all, perhaps sitting still in a chair, never leaving it. Or you may stand or kneel, unfolding your mind to a listening fellow-actor. If the mood is exalted, you may want to lift your arms as you speak. Do so with a great sweeping gesture. Avoid bent elbows, which cramp the grandeur you are trying to express. Use large gestures or none at all.

4. *Presenting the Scene.* When you have brought the scene to performance level, present it on a stage to an audience. While a large stage and a large audience promote vigorous projection, even a small audience and a small stage help the theatrical realization of the scene. The group of actors you belong to, whether drama school students, apprentice actors, community players, or professionals continuing studio training, may present a number of the scenes at one time. Judge the results by audience reaction and by the comments fo a competent critic. Thereafter, rehearse to correct the weaknesses of the scene and to confirm its merits. If possible, offer the scenes again as a second public performance before a larger audience.

SCENES FROM SHAKESPEARE FOR WOMEN AS MAIN CHARACTERS

FROM THE COMEDIES

1. VIOLA and OLIVIA, *Twelfth Night*, I, v, from the entrance of Viola to the end.
2. MRS. PAGE and MRS. FORD, *The Merry Wives of Windsor*, II, i, from the beginning to the entrance of Ford and others.
3. ROSALIND and CELIA, *As You Like It*, III, ii, from the entrance of Rosalind to the entrance of Orlando.
4. MIRANDA, *The Tempest*, III, i, from the entrance of Miranda to the end.
5. HELENA and HERMIA, *A Midsummer Night's Dream*, III, ii, from the entrance of Lysander and Helena to the exit of Helena and Hermia.

6. ARIEL, *The Tempest*, I, ii, from the entrance of Ariel to his exit.

7. TITANIA, *A Midsummer Night's Dream*, II, ii, from the beginning to the exit of Titania.

8. BEATRICE, *Much Ado About Nothing*, IV, ii, from the exit of the Friar and others to the end.

FROM THE HISTORIES

1. LADY PERCY, *Henry IV*, Part I, II; iii.

2. QUEEN ANNE, *Richard II*, III, iv, to the exit of Queen Anne.

3. ANNE BULLEN and an OLD LADY, *Henry VIII*, II, iii.

4. QUEEN KATHARINE, *Henry VIII*, II, iv, to the exit of the Queen and Ladies.

5. ALICE and KATHARINE, *Henry V*, III, iv.

6. HOSTESS and DOLL TEARSHEET, *Henry IV*, Part II, II, iv, from the entrance of the Hostess and Doll Tearsheet to the end.

7. CONSTANCE, *King John*, III, iv, to the exit of Constance.

8. LADY ANNE, *Richard III*, I, ii, to the exit of Lady Anne.

FROM THE TRAGEDIES

1. JULIET and NURSE, *Romeo and Juliet*, II, v.

2. PORTIA, *Julius Caesar*, II, i, from the entrance of Portia to her exit.

3. LADY MACBETH, *Macbeth*, I, v.

4. DESDEMONA and EMILIA, *Othello*, IV, iii.

5. CLEOPATRA, *Antony and Cleopatra*, I, iii.

6. GONERIL, *King Lear*, I, iv, from the entrance of Goneril to the end.

7. VOLUMNIA, *Coriolanus*, III, iii, from the entrance of Volumnia to the end.

8. QUEEN GERTRUDE, *Hamlet*, III, iv.

SCENES FROM SHAKESPEARE FOR MEN AS
MAIN CHARACTERS

FROM THE COMEDIES

1. LANCELOT GOBBO and OLD GOBBO, *The Merchant of Venice*, II, ii, to the entrance of Bassanio and others.

2. LAUNCE, *Two Gentlemen of Verona*, II, iii.

3. TOUCHSTONE and CORIN, *As You Like It*, III, ii, from the entrance of Corin and Touchstone to their exit.

4. FERDINAND, *The Tempest*, III, i.

5. LYSANDER and DEMETRIUS, *A Midsummer Night's Dream*, III, ii, from the entrance of Lysander and Helena to the exit of Helena and Hermia.

6. PROSPERO, *The Tempest*, I, ii, from the entrance of Ariel to the exit of Caliban.

7. OBERON, *A Midsummer Night's Dream*, II, ii, to the entrance of Demetrius and Helena.

8. BENEDICK, *Much Ado about Nothing*, IV, ii, from the exit of the Friar and others to the end.

FROM THE HISTORIES

1. HOTSPUR, *Henry IV*, Part I, II, iii.

2. ARTHUR and HUBERT, *King John*, IV, i.

3. KING HENRY, *Henry V*, IV, iii, from the entrance of King Henry to the entrance of Mountjoy.

4. JOHN OF GAUNT, *Richard II*, II, i, to the exit of John of Gaunt.

5. KING RICHARD II, *Richard II*, IV, i, from the entrance of Richard to the end.

6. FALSTAFF, PISTOL, PRINCE HENRY, *Henry IV*, Part II, II, iv, from the entrance of the Hostess and Doll Tearsheet to the end.

7. WOLSEY, *Henry VIII*, III, ii, from the exit of all but Wolsey to the end.

8. GLOUCESTER, *Richard III*, I, ii, to the end.

FROM THE TRAGEDIES

1. ROMEO, *Romeo and Juliet*, V, iii, to the entrance of Friar Lawrence.
2. BRUTUS and CASSIUS, *Julius Caesar*, IV, iii.
3. MACBETH, *Macbeth*, II, i, to the entrance of the Porter.
4. OTHELLO and IAGO, *Othello*, III, iii, from the exit of Desdemona to her re-entrance.
5. ENOBARBUS, *Antony and Cleopatra*, II, ii, from the exit of Caesar and others to the end.
6. LEAR and the FOOL, *King Lear*, I, iii, from the entrance of the Fool to his exit.
7. CORIOLANUS, *Coriolanus*, V, iii.
8. HAMLET, *Hamlet*, III, iv.

SONNETS FOR STUDY

1. SONNET 42, below, like others in the sequence, reflects the love-triangle of the poet, his friend (probably the young Earl of Southampton), and the Dark Lady. Using pause and emphasis to make its meaning clear, present it as a Shakespearean monologue. Prepare others the same way.

> That thou hast her, it is not all my grief,
> And yet it may be said I lov'd her dearly;
> That she hath thee is of my wailing chief,
> A loss in love that touches me more nearly.
> Loving offenders, thus I will excuse ye:
> Thou dost love her because thou know'st I love her,
> And for my sake even so doth she abuse me,
> Suff'ring my friend for my sake to approve her.
> If I lose thee, my loss is my love's gain,
> And losing her, my friend hath found that loss;
> Both find each other, and I lose both twain,
> And both for my sake lay on me this cross.
>   But here's the joy: my friend and I are one;
>   Sweet flattery! then she loves but me alone.
>
> WILLIAM SHAKESPEARE

2. More sonnets for study appear in Appendices B and C.

11 | ～

Dialects for the Stage

HIGGINS: Now repeat after me, in Hertford,
Hereford and Hampshire, hurricanes hardly
ever happen.
ELIZA: In 'ertford, 'ereford, and 'ampshire,
'urricanes 'ardly hever 'appen.
ALAN JAY LERNER, *My Fair Lady*
(adapted from Shaw's *Pygmalion*)

THE ABILITY TO speak a dialect may be a great asset to an
actor. Stanley Holloway's and Julie Andrews' Cockney
helped to immortalize *My Fair Lady*. Hal Holbrook in
his *Mark Twain Tonight* entertained audiences across the
country with his Southwestern drawl. Maurice Chevalier's
delightful touch of French accent has become his lifelong
trademark. Siobhan McKenna carried her Irish lilt even
into nondialect plays with great success.

There is something indefinably appealing about a true
dialect quality in an appropriate role. Like a half-recog-
nized fragrance, it awakens a memory of other times and
other places. A Yankee twang savors of Down East life
and traditions. Tennessee hillbilly speech calls up the richness of mountain folklore. A Scottish burr invokes Highland hills and mists as "Fi' dullars? It's a bogen" does the
sidewalks of New York. Even more than the sound changes,
the lilt of the dialect stirs such associations in the hearer.
Fortunately for the actor, a playwright who knows the
speech of an area will write with a turn of phrase that
invites its proper lilt. One can almost hear the cadence
of Maurya's "It's a great rest I'll be having now, and its

time, surely," in *Riders to the Sea* or of de Lawd's "Watch yo'sef, Gabe!" in *Green Pastures*.

The acquisition of a dialect for a role is a task that may be required of you as an actor at any time. You may undertake it before you audition for a dialect role. Or, if you are already cast, your director may request it if the spelling used by the playwright suggests it. Dialect spellings are fairly common both in plays and in musical comedies. They serve as guides, though not always as safe ones, to the actor as to the kind and number of changes he should make in assuming the dialect.

Spelling changes, too, are used to suggest foreign accents. All that will be said in this chapter about the acquisition of a dialect applies equally to a foreign accent. The term "accent" has a larger connotation than the word "dialect." It may apply to either cultivated or uncultivated variants of pronunciation. Terms such as "British accent" and "Parisian accent" refer to socially acceptable pronunciations of the English and French languages in these countries. The term "dialect," as used for stage speech especially, carries with it an implication of uncultivated speech and a suggestion that the speech is limited to a locality or region.

The term "American accent," however, as used abroad, is often a term of reproach, implying careless articulation and a nasal twang. The implication is plain in the story of a British actress good at Jewish-Cockney speech who was auditioned in London for a part needing a New York Yiddish quality. The casting director read opposite her in a dialogue which required him to assume the part of a Chinese mandarin. She did her best with the dialect, but the director was not satisfied. "Well, dearie," he said at last, "Your American accent's not so good, is it?" "Neither's your Chinese!" she replied with spirit.

Yet an American accent need not be uneducated. We should defend our best speech as did the New England heroine of Alice Duer Miller's *The White Cliffs*, when her accent was found wanting by Lady Jean, a British aristocrat:

> "You're an American, Miss Dunne?
> Really, you do not speak like one."
> She seemed to think she'd said a thing
> Both courteous and flattering.
> I answered, though my wrists were weak
> With anger, "Not at all. I speak—
> At least, I've always thought this true,—
> As educated people do
> In any country,—even mine."

"American accent," when it is standard, at least, should cultivate self-respect of this kind. It may then hope to win the respect of other brands of English accent, both on the stage and in international forums.

The whole subject of analyzing and synthesizing dialects and accents for stage speech is a large one, needing a book to itself. Spelling alone does not convey the precise pronunciation changes needed. Nor does it convey anything of the most elusive and significant part of a dialect, its speech melody. For these, a knowledge of the International Phonetic Alphabet and of pitch transcription, as described in Chapters 8 and 9, are the best tools. This book will confine itself to an outline of a method of acquiring a stage dialect based on their use.

You will find it easiest to apply the method if you have a good musical ear. A well-developed sense of pitch is almost essential to both the analysis of the inflection patterns of a dialect and the checking of one's own skill in adapting them to the lines of a role. It is important, too, to be consistent throughout. If a vowel or consonant is changed once, as *I* might be changed to *Ah* in Southern speech, it must be changed every time it occurs. The lilt of the dialect also should be used wherever appropriate. In an Irish brogue, a phrase like "It's a grand thing, surely," will always need a dropping inflection on the last word from "sure" to "ly," as well as a trilled *r*.

The first principle of dialect study for the stage is that the actual sound changes of the dialect as spoken are reduced for the sake of comprehensibility. The dialect is simplified, retaining only a few of its variants, generally those that differ most sharply from standard speech. In the case of foreign speech especially, often only a trace of the accent need remain for theatre use. Instead of many sound variants, use shifts in stress from the correct to the wrong syllable of a word, as in French accent one might say, "The price is five doll-ARS." Such shifts, where appropriate, together with minimal vowel and consonant changes and the use of the proper speech melody, will be sufficient to establish the foreign background of the character you are playing.

American dialects you may need include Yankee, Bronx (so-called, really a variant of New York regional speech), Yiddish, Midwestern, and Southern. British stage dialects include Cockney, Irish, and Scottish, usually the Lowland variety. Lancashire and Welsh are occasionally indicated. European "foreign" accents—Italian, German, French, and Spanish—are sometimes called for in British and American plays. We may anticipate the appearance of Asian foreign accents in the future, and of course, Pidgin English has long been with us.

The simplest and best way to acquire a dialect or a foreign accent is to listen to it and imitate it, as one learns a second language in an up-to-date school. Use this method if you possibly can. Start with a dialect or accent with which you already have some familiarity. Perhaps you have heard one used by parents or grandparents; the lilt of such a dialect is already in your ear, and you should be able to reproduce it with great authenticity. Failing this, you may have a favorite comedian whose recordings use the dialect he generally assumes as an entertainer; these recordings would be an excellent source for study of that dialect. If you need to acquire a certain foreign accent, you may know someone from that country whose English is still heavily accented. He may be willing to teach you the accent while you teach him standard pronunciations in exchange.

The method outlined below was developed before the author's *Dialects for the Stage*, offering twenty dialects on cassettes, was published. See the dust jacket of this book. These cassettes make serious attempts at dialect acquisition much easier and quicker. Lacking them, use recordings of the dialect as your main source. A Listening Library of Records (p. 216) lists a few by native speakers in their own dialect, but many are spoken by actors assuming dialect speech that adequately conveys a difference, both regional and cultural, in the speaker.

Steps in the Acquisition of a Stage Dialect

1. ANALYZING A RECORDED DIALECT

Select one or more recordings in which the dialect is used, either by an actor or by one who speaks it naturally. Analyze the dialect by writing in phonetic transcription all words with pronunciations that differ from standard American. Analyze its lilt by dotting in the pitch level of each word on a music staff, using pitch transcription as described in Chapter 9. Write the words below the staff as the words of a song are written below its melody but use phonetic transcription for each of the words in which a dialectal variant occurs.

2. REPRODUCING A RECORDED DIALECT

Reproduce the dialect by saying it aloud exactly as you have transcribed it, both as to the lilt and the pronunciation of the words transcribed in phonetics. Record yourself doing so, and play the recording back to check on its correspondence with the original.

3. SELECTING VARIANTS FOR A STAGE VERSION OF THE DIALECT

List the pronunciation variants you discovered in Step 1, both alphabetically as spelled and phonetically as pronounced in the dialect. Single examples from each of three dialects are shown below.

Bronx: ir as in *first,* ɝ , becomes ɔɪ , fɔɪst
Scottish: r as in *worm,* ɾ , becomes r trilled, ʌ , wɜɾm
French: i as in *hill,* ɪ , becomes i , hil

If you are working from a recording of one who speaks the dialect, decide which variants you will discard to simplify the dialect for stage use. List separately those you decide to retain.

4. APPLYING THE SELECTED VARIANTS TO A ROLE

Study the language of your role. Find and mark every instance in which a sound to be changed into the appropriate variant occurs in the lines. Write above each such word in phonetic transcription both its standard pronunciation and its dialectal pronunciation. Record these words in the dialect, and check by playback for authenticity.

5. APPLYING THE LILT TO A ROLE

Select from the speeches in your role the words, phrases, idioms, and sentences which spring from the dialect you will assume. Especially note any which also occur on your source record or records. Using music staff paper and writing the selections phonetically below the staff, plan inflections for these in pitch transcription, corresponding to the inflection patterns you transcribed in Step 1.

6. PRACTICING SELECTIONS FROM THE ROLE

Read the selections transcribed in Step 5 aloud until the lilt and the pronunciations come easily to you. Add to your phonetic transcription the special symbols for nasality, the glottal shock, lengthened sounds, etc., where these occur. Record these selections, and check by playback for authenticity.

7. RECORDING YOUR ROLE

Practice expanding your use of the dialect to all the lines of your role. Try to drop into the inflection pattern of the lilt wherever possible. Then record your lines, doing the dialogue with a partner who also speaks the dialect, if this is called for. Record yourselves, and check by comparing the naturalness of your dialect with that on the source record.

8. APPLYING THE DIALECT TO OTHER MATERIAL

Using the pronunciations and the lilt spontaneously, apply the dialect to any material in English, in or out of a dialectal context. See the examples of different dialect readings of the lines "This above all," etc., at the end of this chapter.

9. AD LIBBING IN THE DIALECT

Ad lib in the dialect, improvising a scene with a partner who does the same. Strive for easy naturalness, checking on the changes you make by ear.

The above process may seem very laborious. If, however, you have any natural facility for dialects, you will pass quite rapidly to Steps 7, 8, and 9. You should return to the earlier steps if your success is uneven at first. When you can undertake Step 9 readily, you may consider that you are near mastery of the dialect. You should then be able to use it in rehearsal without fear of sounding unnatural or affected.

In any case, you should resolve to master a dialect or not attempt it at all. Inconsistent changes sound peculiar even to a member of the audience unfamiliar with the dialect. Nothing is more absurd in some amateur productions than a half-hearted late attempt to get something like a Scottish dialect, for instance, by merely burring an r now and then. To the knowing ear, inconsistencies sound ridiculous and tend to destroy the reality of the character instead of heightening it. If you do decide to learn a dialect, do not neglect the lilt. Even a trace of accent, accompanied by its true lilt, is more convincing than all the sound changes without it.

A good dialect can enhance more than the modern play where it has been written in. Directors often call for a dialect, usually Cockney, for the low-life characters in Shakespeare's plays. Falstaff's companions, the mechanics of *A Midsummer Night's Dream*, or the gravediggers in *Hamlet* may use a broad Cockney that makes them entirely familiar to a London audience. American directors might use the same device. Why not a gravedigger with a Bronx dialect?

"Here loys the pernt; if I draown moiself wittin'ly, it awgues an ack; and an ack hat' t'ree branches, it is to ack, to do, and to poifo-em; argal, she draowned herself wittin'li."

hɪr lɔɪz ðə pɜrnt; ɪf ɑɪ dræ͌ʊn mɔɪˈsʌlf ˈwɪtn̩lɪ, ɪt ˈɔqjuz ən ˀæk; n̩ n̩ ˀæk hæˈtri ˈbræ͌ntʃəz, ɪt ɪz tə ˀæk, tə du, ən tə pɔɪfoəm; ɔqæ͌l, ʃi dræ͌ʊnd hɔɪˈsʌlf ˈwɪtn̩lɪ.

(Note how writing out the dialect in IPA enables one to reproduce the sound changes which make it authentic but which cannot be reproduced in spelling, such as nasality and the glottal shock.)

One word of warning to the actor who has great facility with an accent or dialect; it may win you a role in a professional production, but it may also tie you to such roles thereafter. The risk, however, may be well worth taking to get started. Explore your potential with the exercises below, and if it is marked, develop it accordingly. Even if it is not, the next chapter, on reading aloud, auditioning, and performing, is for you. If you have developed your best tone, articulation, and flexibility in working through the earlier chapters, these final steps you are soon to take should lead you nearer to success in the theatre.

Exercises for Developing Facility in a
Dialect for the Stage

1. Select a role from one of the plays in Group 1 below, in each of which the playwright indicates dialect changes by spelling changes. Using appropriate records from the list in the Appendix and any other sources available to you, work through the steps outlined above before memorizing the lines. Follow the variants on the records you are using rather than the playwright's spelling.

2. Select a role from any of the plays in Group 2 below, in most of which no spelling changes have been made but in which the locale of the play and its content make a dialect quality appropriate in the speech of one or more characters. Work through each step as before.

3. Choosing any low-life character in an Elizabethan or Restoration play, apply to it the uncultivated pronunciations of the region where you were born and brought up. For example, you might try Mrs. Page or Mrs. Ford of *The Merry Wives of Windsor* in Yankee or Midwestern speech. Teach the regionalisms to a fellow-actor who will work at the scene with you, using enough changes to achieve a local quality. Present the scene on the stage for the edification and amusement of your friends or fellow-actors.

TWELVE READINGS IN VARIOUS REGIONAL AND
DIALECTAL PRONUNCIATIONS

> This above all; to thine own self be true,
> And it must follow, as the night the day
> Thou canst not then be false to any man.
>
> POLONIUS, *Hamlet*

The quotation appears twelve times in the following pages in the kinds of speech listed below. Pronunciations are shown in phonetic transcription and the lilt in pitch transcription.

1. Standard American speech

ðıs ə-ˈbʌv ɔl tə ðaın on self bi tru   ænd ıt mʌst ˈfalo æz ðə naıt ðə de

ðav kænst nat ðɛn bi fɔls tu ˈɛn-ı mæn

2. Regional New York City speech

ðıs ə-bʌv ɔːl tə ðaın on ˈsɛ-ɔlf bi tru æ̆nd ıt mʌst ˈfalo æz ðə naıt ðə de.

ðæ̆v kæ̆nst nat ðɛn bi fals tv ˈɛ̄n-ı mæ̆n

3. Southern Virginia speech

ðıs ə-ˈbʌv ol tə ðaɹn on sʌlf bı tru æn ıt mʌs ˈfɔ-lo ǣz ðə naːıt ðɘ deı

ðav ˈke-ɘɹt ðɛn bı fɔls tə ˈɛɹ mæn

4. Standard British speech

ðıs ə-ˈbʌv ɔːl tə ðaın on sɛlf bi tru   ænd ıt mʌst ˈfɒ-lo æz ðə naıt ðe deı

ðav kænst nɒt ðɛn bı fɔls tu ˈɛn-ı mæn

5. Cockney speech

ðıs ə-ˈbʌv ɔl tu ðaın hon sʌlf bı tru hæn ıt mʌs ˈfɔ-lo hæz ðə naıʔ ðə deı

ðæ̆v kæ̆nst nɒʔ ðɛn bı fɔls tu ˈhɛ-nı mæn

6. Irish speech

ðıs ə-'bʌv ɔl tə ðaın oːn sɛlf bı θru æn ıt mʌst 'fɒ-lo æz ðə naıt ðə deː

ðav kænst nɒt ðın bı fɒls tu 'ɪn-ı man

7. Scottish (Lowland) speech

ðıs ə-'bun ɔl tə ðan oːn sɛlf bı tɹu æn ıt mʊst 'fɒ-lo az ðə naʔ ðə deı

ðav 'ka-nə ðɛn bı fɒls tə 'ɒn-ı mɒn

8. Welsh speech

ðɛsː ə-bʌv ɔːl tu ðan on sɛlf bı tru æn ıt mʌst fɒ-lo az ðə naıt ðə deː

ðav kænst nat ðɛn bı fɒlsː tu ɛn-ı mæn

9. Northern British (Lancashire) speech

ðıs ə-bʊv ɔl tu ðaım oːn sɛlf bı tru ænd ıt mʊst fɒ-lo az ðə naıt ðə de

ðav kanst nɒt ðɛn bı fɒls tu ɛn-ı man

10. Yiddish speech

ðıs ə-bʌv ɒl tu ðaın on sɛlf bı tru ænd ıt mʌst fa-lo az ðə naː ðə deːı

ðav kænst nat ðɛn bı fɒls tu ɛn-ı mæn

11. Italian speech

ðıs ə-bʌv ɔːl tə ðaın on-ə sɛlf-ə bı tru ænd ıt mʌst-ə fa-lo əz ðə naıt-ə ðə deːı

ðav kænst nat ðɛn-ə bı fɔls-ə tu ɛn-ı mæn

12. Standard Canadian speech

ðıs ə-bʌv ɔl tu ðaın on sɛlf bı tru ænd ıt mʌst fa-lo əz ðə naıt ðə de

ðav kænst nat ðɛn bı fɔls tu ɛn-ı mæn

Two groups of plays using dialects.

GROUP 1

Play	Author	Follow spelling changes for dialects listed
Bus Stop	William Inge	Southern Western
The Green Pastures	Marc Connelly	Southern
In White America	Martin Duberman	Southern
My Sister Eileen	Joseph Fields and Jerome Chodorov	New York
Major Barbara	George Bernard Shaw	Cockney
The Homecoming	Harold Pinter	Cockney
Hamlet of Stepney Green	Bernard Copps	East London
Shadow and Substance	Paul Vincent Carroll	Irish
The Old Lady Shows Her Medals	J. M. Barrie	Scottish Cockney
Armstrong's Last Goodnight	John Arden	Scottish
The Waters of Babylon	John Arden	North British Irish East London Central European
Anastasia	Guy Bolton	Russian

GROUP 2

Play	Author	Make sound changes appropriate for dialects listed
Our Town	Thornton Wilder	New England
A Raisin in the Sun	Lorraine Hansberry	Black American
Inherit the Wind	Jerome Lawrence and Robert E. Lee	Southern
Summer and Smoke	Tennessee Williams	Southern
Pygmalion	George Bernard Shaw	English cultivated Cockney
Sergeant Musgrave's Dance	John Arden	British (various)
Riders to the Sea	John M. Synge	Irish

The ballad below, spoken in a rich native Highland Scots dialect, may be heard on one of the cassettes in the author's *Dialects for the Stage*. Hearing it may convince you that listening is the best way to learn a dialect.

From TRUE THOMAS, A SCOTTISH BALLAD

True Thomas lay on Huntley Bank,
A fairlie [1] he spied with his e'ee.
And there he saw a lady bright
Come riding doon by the Eildon Tree.

Her skirt was o' the grassgreen silk,
Her mantle o' the velvet fine,
At ilka tet [2] o' her horse's mane
Hung fifty siller bells and nine . . .

"Harp and carp,[3] Thomas", she said,
"Harp and carp along wi' me.
And if ye dare to kiss my lips,
Sure of your body I shall be."

"Betide me weel, betide me woe,
That weird shall never daunten me!"
Syne he has kissed her rosy lips
All underneath the Eildon Tree . . .

[1] fairlie: fairy   [2] ilka tet: every braid   [3] carp: chat

12 | ~

Reading Aloud, Auditioning, and Performing

Fame is the spur that the clear spirit doth raise,
(That last infirmity of noble mind,)
To scorn delights and live laborious days.

MILTON, *Lycidas*

THE YOUNG ACTOR is always an impatient person. He wants to begin acting on the first day of his training. He feels, perhaps rightly, that a great talent was born in him, and that the world is waiting for it. He can already speak and move; therefore, let him act!

But the "divine power to speak words" comes only after "long trial," as Walt Whitman has said. In a school of acting or a university drama department, acting and speech are studied and practiced concurrently. You may be using your speech to act with while it is still being developed. You may appear in classroom scenes and have as well the opportunity to audition for roles in full-length plays. Your first reading is always of the greatest importance. You must make a good impression then if you are to be called back for a second reading. The moment you open your mouth, your speech will have its effect, helping or hindering your chances. As you read on, you must display your powers of speech easily and confidently, as well as relating them to the role you hope to win. You must, in fact, be a good oral reader.

This chapter, therefore, will consider first the art of reading aloud. Good oral reading, whether for an audition or for any other purpose, results from the use of good speech itself, to which are added three things: the leading eye, the recurring pause, and the telling inflection. The basic necessity, of course, is the use of all the techniques of good speech while reading—complete relaxation, pleasant tone, clear articulation, and ample variety. Beginning with relaxation, as described in Chapter 5, you must apply them to oral reading, both prepared and at sight. If, in the latter, you can bring them to bear instantly, as soon as you recognize the meanings of the words on the page, your speech in reading will be lively and natural. Your nervousness will tend to disappear, there will be no monotony, and the listener's ear should be pleased at the same time as his mind is engaged.

Good speech alone, however, does not make one a good reader. Oral reading involves the simultaneous use of the eye, the ear, and the voice, all coordinated by the brain. It is this triple aspect of the operation that has to be mastered. Silent-reading skills, used so frequently by us all, arouse inner speech, the speech of thought, not outer speech, the speech of sound. When we read aloud, silent-reading habits tend to dominate because they are so familiar. This dominance must be overcome. Silent-reading habits must be adjusted to meet the needs of the processes of speech. In reading aloud, the brain receives the words through the eye and directs the muscles of speech to form them in sounds. The ear hears these sounds and feeds them back to the brain via the hearing nerve. Their arrival signifies that the operation called for has been successfully carried out. Meanwhile, the eye is picking up more words with which to continue the reading. This goes on and on, each part of the process triggering the next, in a circle of stimulus-response-action issuing in continuous speech.

The *leading eye* is so called in oral reading because it is precisely that. It looks down at the text and out at the audience by turns. The actor who is a good oral reader looks up constantly from his book, like a broadcaster on television making eye contact with his hearers or an actor with his partner in a dialogue that is being read for a role. He avoids any breaks in the material, which seems to be memorized because it flows along so easily. This skill—easy, frequent looking up from the page—is an uncommon one. Practiced public speakers have learned it as a matter of survival, for he who reads a speech with his eyes fixed on the typewritten page inevitably makes a poor impression on his audience. Even the college professor who reads his lectures rather than speaking them might not survive except for the fact that he has a captive audience. Secretaries reading minutes are rarely listened to as they monotone along, never looking up. Report-reading, if carried out in the same way, suffers the same fate. Speakers on television have learned how essential it is to look at the camera, so that the audience may experience a direct eye contact with them. They are helped out by the teleprompter, which runs along at eye level, presenting in a moving sequence the words they must speak, thus making it unnecessary for them to look at a page. But the viewer can always tell when the speaker's eyes are fixed on this "idiot board."

Even if as an actor you do use it for a television appearance, you must learn the leading-eye skill for all other reading-aloud situations. This makes it possible for you to read any printed material at sight directly, looking at the hearers, dropping your eyes to the paper only occasionally and briefly. The reading seems spontaneous; the material can be made to seem your own. You are brought at once into direct contact with your audience or with your fellow-actors in an audition. In the latter case, you may be able to speak the lines as though you were already acting them. This of itself makes it easier to inflect them naturally. By contrast, reading with your eyes on the page keeps you shut in a private world which does not relate closely to your hearers.

The effort to tear one's eyes away from the page is always great at first. Yet you must make the attempt. You must realize that you are going to take the words into your mind, look up from the page, speak them to the audience, and then look down for more. You must, if need be, wrench your eyes away from the text to create direct speaker-to-listener communication. It is the snatching up of words into the mind that is the clue. As the last of these words are spoken, drop your eyes to the page again and sweep up into your memory another half-line. Cover this break by sustaining a vowel very slightly in a final syllable or by pausing for a second at a useful comma, taking a breath if need be or slowing your speed a little. Thus, you may give yourself a fraction of a second for each swoop of the eyes down to the page for the capture of enough words to refuel your speech so that it may drive on without a break.

The hardest thing to learn is the widened eye span. The eye must be able to read five or more words at a glance, widening its span from the two or three words which may have been its limit previously. For some, because of their natural reading habits, this comes more easily than for others. If it is difficult to acquire, you should find a good speed-reading textbook and practice its exercises. Proper timing must be learned too, since it requires nice judgment to determine at what point the leading eye must break from the audience and become the reading eye, while the voice continues to speak. The timing must be so skillful that the two are kept in tandem, the eye always ahead of the voice.

You may test yourself in this at once. Take any clearly printed material, preferably on a subject interesting to you, and begin to read it aloud. If you do not have anyone to read to, read to your mirror and be your own audience. Sit, for greater relaxation, with your book in hand, held well up in front of your chin so that you can see your face in the mirror. As you read, look up and catch your own eyes at least once on every line. If necessary, drag your eyes away from the page and speak to your image or to your listeners as long as the words in your mind last. Then calmly look back at the page in relaxed silence. Finding your place, span the line with your eye, catching up into your mind as many words as you can, and resume your speaking aloud. When you reach the end of a line, swing your eyes back to the left margin of the type, as in rapid reading, while in the very act of speaking the last words of the previous line. Look up again and continue as before. Speak as much as possible directly to the listeners, looking one and all firmly in the eye. Stanislavski, in *An Actor's Handbook,* speaks of "giving out and receiving rays . . . invisible currents which we use to communicate with one another." Something of this sort happens as you look right at your hearers while you read to them. When you return to your page for more words, let your audience wait, if need be, while your eye gathers a fresh phrase. This down, up-and-on, down again sequence becomes rhythmic, easy, and unhurried. The listeners have plenty to think about, since your last sentence is still ringing in their ears. Pause is for them not a liability but an asset.

This kind of *recurring pause* is the second virtue in reading aloud. Listeners do not have a text in their hands. They are utterly dependent upon the sounds of the words they hear for the sense of the reading. They must catch the meaning immediately, during the brief time the words just spoken linger in their minds. Words and meanings are either grasped then or they go by, never to be caught again. Frequent comfortable pauses by the reader give the listeners some hope of retaining what has just been said long enough to relate it to the whole scheme of the narrative. Words are the food of the brain, and if the ear receives its food as the mouth does, in small amounts, with pauses in between for swallowing, as it were, the brain may ingest them and assimilate them more fully.

Sometimes a reader's pause is unintentional, occurring because he has lost his place. If this happens to you, remain unperturbed, and your audience will not mind the brief delay. There is actually a kind of stimulus about pause. It has a dramatic value, one an actor soon feels and recognizes. It points up the force of what has just been said. It also maintains suspense as to what is to come next. One young contender for a poetry-speaking prize won it by a fluke and never forgot the value of pause thereafter. The poem was Alfred Noyes's "Burial of a Queen." The critical verse ran:

They should have left her in the vineyards, left her heart to her
  land's own keeping,
Left her white breast room to breathe, and left her white foot free
  to dance!
Hush! Between the solemn pinewoods, carry the lovely lady
  sleeping
Out of the cold grey Northern mists, with banner and scutcheon,
  plume and lance.

Enjoying the rich sentimentality of the verse, she spoke the lines fervently, aware that the audience was listening attentively. Gratified by their interest, her mind wandered from its concentration on the poem itself. She arrived at the word "Hush" and spoke it like a command. The audience hushed obediently and waited. Nothing more happened. Her mind had suddenly gone blank. In silence she gazed at the audience and they at her. The pause seemed endless. Just as she was about to give up in despair, back to her mind flashed the last half of the line, "carry the lovely lady sleeping." She delivered it with the emphasis of immense relief and continued to the end. When she had finished, to her amazement, there was prolonged applause. The silence had filled the gap left by the forgotten half-line, and no one had recognized her plight. The audience believed the pause was for effect.

The final technique that you must learn is how to use *telling inflection*. Make of inflection a kind of warning system, suggesting to the hearer what may be ahead. Keep accommodating it to the text, adjusting it on the fly, so to speak, to tie the words now on your lips into the meaning of the next words that will spring into your eye from the page. You may think of this as a kind of open-end procedure, often accomplished by using an upward inflection as memory runs out of words. The slight rise suggests that there is a new idea still to come. Conversely, when you are in the middle of a sentence and do not know where it will lead, you must keep the inflection uncommitted. You should read easily along, keeping the pitch fairly level, letting it rise as a phrase is ending, to provide a springboard into the next phrase. Eyes on your hearers most of the time, you continuously adjust the inflection to carry forward the sense of the sentence. As you see the end of a sentence or paragraph approaching, you begin to drop your pitch in a way that suggests the close of a thought. If, however, the sentence ends in a query, you may raise the pitch sharply to indicate a question. At all times it will be moving freely, ready to give emphasis at any moment to whatever important word or phrase shows up. It is telling inflection in two ways. In the idiomatic sense, it gives words extra significance. In the direct sense, it literally tells the hearers what they may expect the thought to do next.

Oral reading practice, especially sight-reading practice, needs to begin early in your speech training program because of its complexity. You may begin with material from plays, both familiar and unfamiliar, since you are preparing yourself for auditions. Start with shorter speeches and easier dialogue (if you are working with a partner) and continue with longer and longer speeches, ultimately those of Shaw and Shakespeare. Set up a tape recorder to tell you at playback whether you have succeeded in creating an illusion of complete familiarity with the text. After a first reading and playback, note the breaks in the continuity and any ill-assorted inflection patterns; then leave that speech and go on to another. You are practicing sight-reading now, and by following this method, you will repeatedly subject yourself to the same difficulties and discover the way through them. Finally, you should use the technique with completely unfamiliar material. For fun, read at sight to young children, choosing lively poems and stories with a climax. Enchant them with huge melodramatic inflections: "And THEN the wolf jumped *right* out of bed. 'HELP!' screamed Red Riding Hood. . . ." Your audience will hang on your words.

Six weeks to six months of such practice should make you an accomplished sight-reader. It will prove a skill that will help you to face many tasks confidently but particularly that most important of all reading-aloud situations for you, the audition for a part in a play. The audition is a barrier through which you must break if you are to get a chance to act. In a nonprofessional audition, the play and the role you want to read for are often known to you in advance. Study both thoroughly, familiarizing yourself with all the lines the character speaks throughout the play, not just those you may read at the audition. You may then expect to be at ease in the part, able to apply to the audition the reading-aloud techniques you have learned. You use the leading eye to make and keep contact with any actor sharing the scene with you and to keep your mind ahead of your voice so that you pick up cues almost as fast as in a performance. You use recurring pause where the sense allows it in your speeches. Your inflections should accommodate themselves to whatever reading your partner gives to a cue line. You should thus be able to give a fluent, easy reading, in which all the voice qualities you have learned and some attributes of the character you hope to play may be easily apparent.

You may someday get a chance to read for a part in a new play, or if the need for a sudden replacement arises, you may be called upon to read lines at sight. If you have practiced reading aloud as suggested in this chapter, you will have nothing to fear. The calmness of mind which helps an audition may be induced by your inner assurance that you can read well anything written in English, whether you have seen it before or not, even if you do not fully understand it. It is entirely possible that a listener may apprehend more of a new play at its first reading than the actors do, just as on an unfamiliar road a passenger in an automobile sees and enjoys more of the scenery than does the driver. The mind of the driver is taken up with the mechanics of driving and steering the car. Your mind likewise will be driving your well-trained speech and steering your inflections along new roads of thought unfolding in the text before you. The exercises for the relaxation of your vocal tract in Chapter 5 will help relax you for the ordeal. Secure in your habitual control of whatever you read aloud, you are master of the process. If you are lucky in other respects, you very likely will be awarded the coveted role.

When you enter upon rehearsal with the director and the cast, you will go through a first reading of the play. Now you can sense your relationship to the other characters and the interpretation of them by the other actors and find out if there are any special speech requirements for you—an uneducated quality or a dialect or a foreign accent. If so, you should begin to work on it at once, so that it may quickly become part and parcel of the role.

In the first weeks of rehearsal, the director is blocking out the action and indicating how each character should be developed. As soon as these outlines are clear, you may safely learn your lines. You should avoid any set readings at this time. The special inflection that a critical line may need will develop as the scene is worked and reworked by the actors to the director's satisfaction. It will be part of the dynamics of the whole scene and part of the expression of the character.

You yourself must take care of any problems of projection and articulation which arise during rehearsal in relation to your role. You should always make sure that your voice carries to the rear of the orchestra and to the top of the balcony. It is much easier for a director to call for a reduction of volume than to prod an inaudible actor into greater efforts. It may be true of projection that, as George Papashvily's uncle said of the wedding feast in *Anything Can Happen*, only too much is enough!

Difficulties in articulation may lie hidden in innocent-looking lines. If you find that you stumble repeatedly over a certain phrase, it probably contains a problem in the awkward juxtaposition of sounds, as in the line "The Leith police dismisseth us." The lip-whisper-say method described in Chapter 8 will isolate the difficult movement sequence, allowing slow practice of the core of the stumbling block. In the example above, practice of "misseth us" by itself, tongue-tip in, out, in, for *s, th, s*, helps solve the problem. In each case, once the movements are correct, the sounds become clear.

Care of your voice through the rehearsal and perform-

ance period of the play is your responsibility. If you feel
that you are getting a cold or sore throat, you should take
a day off at once, resting completely. This may be your
only chance of preventing the cold from developing. It is
wise then to speak softly in all rehearsals. You can explain
the problem to your director, who will be only too anxious
to promote your recovery. If you realize that the vocal
cords are actually inflamed when the throat is sore and
that using them in speech may harm them as running
would a sprained ankle, you may be willing to give them
the rest they must have in order to recover.

As soon as the play has reached the point at which
run-throughs begin, the actors should warm up their
voices before going on the stage, using the Actor's Warm-
up Exercises at the end of this book. On the opening
night of a play, especially if it is a Shakespearean or
Restoration drama, with great demands on speech, the
actors should carry out a complete set of tone and articulation exercises to allow them to say their opening lines
in full voice. A strong beginning, with clear voices resounding easily through the theatre, immediately creates
a responsive audience and gets the play off to a good
start.

A college play may run for only a few nights, and the
cast may just be settling down into a comfortable performance when the show is over. The actors will get no more
than a taste of the security of a successful run, with satis-
factory readings of difficult lines, timing for laughs
smoothed out, and speech and action climaxes integrated.
The first time, however, that you do experience a long
run, you may find that your voice is remarkably robust.
If speech is properly produced, you can carry a long role
night after night, with benefit rather than strain to your
speech mechanism. Like any muscles, those of the speaking voice grow stronger and improve their coordination

with constant use. Besides, your ear is nightly experiencing the wider range of pitch change and the more subtle use of inflection which characterize speech on the stage. This in turn has a beneficial effect on your own.

Throughout your theatre career, you should continue to work on your voice and speech. You must always regard it as an instrument on which you play and of which you must be the master. Your techniques, if faithfully practiced, will slowly increase your total speech powers. When you feel a great confidence in your ability to utter the words as their sense and sound require, you have achieved the first goal of speech training for the stage, the mastery of the vocal techniques of production and projection. But this mastery must be maintained by continuing to work off the stage as well as on.

The last achievement that you should seek is a different matter. It is complementary to the physical approach to speech which may seem to dominate this book. It is exemplified in the story Margaret Webster tells of the founder and director of the original Old Vic company, Lilian Baylis. She once asked Charles Laughton, then a newcomer to the company, if he felt able to act a Shakespearean role. "Madam," replied Laughton, "I sleep with a copy of *Hamlet* under my pillow." "Ah," came the reply, "But can you speak his lovely words?"

What she demanded was joy in the spoken word, a delight in utterance, springing from mastery of vocal techniques, combined with devotion to great language, a homage and a dedication that adds a richness and a glow to theatre speech. This over-plus, this superabundance of beauty and power in words spoken, has its source in the actor's mind and spirit. He feels within him the greatness of what he is to say, he knows that his body as a speech instrument is ready and able to fulfil his demands, and in a kind of exaltation he hears himself rising to the heights of eloquence and passion that the words and the action require. He senses that he dominates the stage and that the audience is being moved to ecstasy, to pity or terror by what they hear or see. The play has come to life, and the syllables that are spoken are more than mere words. They are the utterances of a human spirit, released by the dramatist and by the actor to speak for once with a universal voice and to create a moment of theatre that will endure.

Your speech as an actor on the stage is truly more than the sum of its parts. Throughout your professional life you must continue to develop your control of breathing, to amplify your resonance, to widen your pitch range, and to sharpen your articulation. But beyond all this you have another task to fulfill, which may be a lifelong effort. It is nothing less than the mastery of your mother tongue, English, its sense and its sound. When you are at ease among words, you should be able to make your speech an instrument of total communication of the thinking, feeling, and willing of a character in a play at a high moment in its history. It is this special quality that makes a listener remember for years certain speeches of an actor, those that "rose with him, flowering in their melting snow," to borrow from another context Dylan Thomas' extraordinary line. This quality defies analysis, but it is of the very essence of theatre. It raises the actor from the status of a craftsman to that of a creative artist.

As such, it is important that you should understand the relation of your skills in theatre speech and movement to your creative art. The relation is that of servants to a master. A servant must be skilled to do his master's bidding, to supply his every need and fulfill his every wish. In the same way, speech and movement should serve acting. The body must present your role visually, whether you are moving about, standing or sitting, leaning or lying prone. Arms, legs, head, and trunk should express much of your meaning in large movement or subtle gesture. Your speech likewise must be a servant of the acting. It must follow the lead of your highest consciousness, which is absorbed in the role you are playing. Your speech will move faster or slower, grow louder or softer, range higher or lower, according to the dictates of the acting. Like faithful retainers, well-trained and kept long in service, speech and movement remain disciplined and trustworthy, obedient to the actor in performance. Even when he himself is exhausted, when the freshness of a role is spent, and the acting of a part seems utterly wearisome, they may continue to function serviceably, and to sustain the acting which first molded them into the form they have taken. At such times you may lean on the old behaviorist theory of emotions—that we are sorry because we cry, frightened because we run, and, one might add, exalted because we declaim!

It may perhaps be presumptuous for a speech teacher to suggest how you may prepare yourself for the great moments of creation on the stage. You may have to wait until long experience of life and of acting bring you to such fruition. In the meantime, however, as a lover of language and a craftsman of the spoken word, you can stretch your horizons to enclose more literature and a wider vocabulary. If you are pursuing academic studies and your professional training at the same time, as is often the case, your reading courses should all be grist to your mill. Not only dramatic literature, but poetry, biography, fiction, history, and philosophy can deepen your knowledge of language and of life. At the same time, your work with speech techniques will relate to the literature you are studying. The associations that cluster round words and phrases will enrich your understanding of the lines you will speak and in some measure suggest how you should say them. Your intellectual concepts of language will fuse with your physical mastery of speech techniques to give you full freedom of speech on the stage.

With such training, if you are English, you will be ready to enter into your heritage of good theatre speech. If you are Canadian, you will draw both from British brilliance and American ease to establish a speech separate from either yet acceptable to both. If you are American, you may at length break with a lingering tradition—the tradition that American actors speak badly on the stage. Their speech, in fact, has been too long in disrepute. It has variously been called lazy-lipped, inaudible, undistinguished, and much more. This situation is changing. Some American actors have always had distinguished speech, and slowly, as here and there young actors emerge from the newer training grounds for the theatre, they bring with them clear and incisive speech. It is rich, powerful, and dynamic for the classic theatre, relaxed in quality, casual in inflection for a realistic play, sharp and cutting for the "theatre of the absurd," so that the words at least are clear though the play's meaning may be obscure. These actors use standard American pronunciation, recognizing that British variants are no more appropriate here than American usage would be in London or Winnipeg or Melbourne. They avoid regionalisms but do not try to strip the speech of a continent down to the bare bones of a rigid conformity.

You, as an English-speaking student of acting, and indeed of any form of speech for public use, may take heart from this situation. You belong to an age when the spoken word of the living actor, televised or on the stage, is regaining the ground once lost to radio and movies. On the North American continent and in Australia, a single language prevails from coast to coast. And this is the language that in the future may dominate international television. Eventually the newscaster, the statesman, and the actor may all expect world audiences. Many varieties of English speech will grow familiar here and abroad, and we shall at length grow tolerant of varying pronunciations of common words. Clarity, beauty, and naturalness rather than uniformity will be the open sesame for you as an English-speaking actor, wherever you were born. Readying your speech to meet these challenges, for such a future and for such an audience you must prepare.

A SHORT GUIDE TO SIGHT-READING PRACTICE

1. Recognize the *faults* of poor sight-reading:
   a. Eyes are on the book, not on the audience.
   b. Voice is often a mumble.
   c. Pitch is usually monotonous.

2. Recognize the *reasons* for these faults:
   a. Fear of losing one's place.
   b. Fear of stumbling in one's speech.
   c. Fear of being ridiculous.

3. Correct these faults:
   a. Select the right fear, the fear of being *dull*.
   b. Hold interest of audience by being the reverse of dull—highly stimulating.
   c. Achieve this by
      (1) Keeping the eye *ahead of the voice*, slowing down, if necessary, *within*, not *between* words. Do this by sustaining long vowels and nasals.
      (2) Using pauses, bits of silence, so the audience can take in what you have just said.
      (3) Using an open-end inflection at a line's or page's end, to continue naturally.
      (4) Keeping aware of the triple nature of the act: the eye, the voice, and the ear working together.
      (5) Reading aloud before a mirror daily.

A Listening Library of Records

Abbreviations. A & M: A & M, Bud: Buddah, Caed: Caedmon, Cap: Capitol, CMS: CMS, Col: Columbia, CSP: Columbia Special Products, Folk: Folkways, Mark: Mark, Pol: Polydor, Sp Arts: Spoken Arts. Many of the selections below are also on cassettes. Consult current catalogues.

American Actors and Actresses

PERFORMER	RECORD TITLE	AUTHOR	RECORD LABEL
Jane Alexander	Mourning Becomes Electra	Eugene O'Neill	Caed TRS 345
Mildred Dunnock	Death of a Salesman	Arthur Miller	Caed TRS 310
Tammy Grimes	Higgledy Piggledy Pop	Maurice Sendak	Caed TC 1519
	A Rose for Emily	Wm. Faulkner	Caed TC 1638
Uta Hagen	Othello	Shakespeare	CSP CSL 153
	Who's Afraid of Virginia Woolf?	Edward Albee	CSP CDOS 687
Katharine Hepburn	A Delicate Balance	Edward Albee	Caed TRS 360
Julie Harris	The Glass Menagerie	Tennessee Williams	Caed TRS 301
Lee Remick	A Delicate Balance	Edward Albee	Caed TRS 360
Original Cast	For Colored Girls Who Have Considered Suicide When the Rainbow Is Enuf	K. Shange	Bud 95007

John Barrymore	*Shakespeare Soliloquies*	Shakespeare	AudioRarities 2280/2281
Ed Begley	*Great American Speeches*		Caed TC 2031
Douglas Campbell	*Oedipus Rex*	Sophocles	Caed TC 2012
Lee J. Cobb	*Death of a Salesman*	Arthur Miller	Caed TRS 310
Joseph Cotten	*A Delicate Balance*	Edward Albee	Caed TRS 360
Henry Fonda	*The Grapes of Wrath*	John Steinbeck	Caed TC 1570
José Ferrer	*Othello*	Shakespeare	CSP CSL 153
Bert Lahr	*Waiting for Godot*	Samuel Beckett	Caed TRS 352
E. G. Marshall	*Great American Speeches*		Caed TC 2031
Zero Mostel	*Rhinoceros*	Eugene Ionesco	Caed TRS 364
Vincent Price	*Great American Poetry*		Caed TC 2009
Paul Robeson	*Othello*	Shakespeare	CSP CSL 153
Original Cast	*The Boys in the Band*	M. Crowley	A&M 6001

British Actors and Actresses

PERFORMER	RECORD TITLE	AUTHOR	RECORD LABEL
Claire Bloom	*Silver Pennies*	B. Thompson, ed.	Caed TC 1495
Maggie Smith	*The Master Builder*	Henrik Ibsen	Caed TRS 307
Vanessa Redgrave	*Twelfth Night*	Shakespeare	Caed SRS 213
Margaret Webster	*Othello*	Shakespeare	CSP CSL 153
Irene Worth	*Happy Days*	Samuel Beckett	Caed TRS 366
Dame Judith Anderson	*Medea*	Euripides	Caed TRS 302
Dame Edith Evans	*Homage to Shakespeare*	Shakespeare	CSP 91A 02048
	Eighteenth Century Comedy	Congreve, Farquhar	HLM 7108°

°Distributed by EMI Records, Ltd., Hayes, Middlesex, England.

Dame Flora Robson	The Family Reunion	T. S. Eliot	Caed TRS 308
Dame Sybil Thorndike	The Family Reunion	T. S. Eliot	Caed TRS 308
	Henry VIII, Excerpts	Shakespeare	Sp Arts 881
Albert Finney	Romeo and Juliet	Shakespeare	Caed SRS 228
Boris Karloff	Just-So Stories	R. Kipling	Caed TC 1038
Alec McGowen	Saint Joan	G. B. Shaw	Argo ZPR 119
	Importance of Being Earnest	Oscar Wilde	Caed TRS 329
Paul Scofield	Twelfth Night	Shakespeare	Caed SRS 213
	Macbeth	Shakespeare	Caed SRS 231
Sir John Gielgud	Ages of Man	Shakespeare	CSP 91A 02056, also Caed SRS 200
	Hamlet (excerpts)	Shakespeare	CSP ADOS 702
Lord Laurence Olivier	Homage to Shakespeare	Shakespeare	CSP 91A 02048
Sir Michael Redgrave	Pygmalion	G. B. Shaw	Caed TRS 354
	The Tempest	Shakespeare	Caed SRS 201
Sir Ralph Richardson	The . Poetry of Keats	John Keats	Caed TC 1087
	Julius Caesar	Shakespeare	Caed SRS 230
	Cyrano de Bergerac	Edmond Rostand	Caed TRS 306
	Soul of an Age	Shakespeare	Caed TC 1170

Humor

PERFORMER	RECORD TITLE	AUTHOR	RECORD LABEL
Victor Borge	Caught in the Act		CSP CCL 646
Stan Freberg	Best of Radio Shows		Cap SM 2020
Hermione Gingold	Lysistrata	Aristophanes	Caed TRS 313
Stanley Holloway	Nonsense Verse	Lear, Carroll	Caed TC 1087
Lily Tomlin	& That's		Pol 5023
Flip Wilson	Funny and Live		Sp Arts 4004

Poetry Readings, Documentaries, Tongue Twisters

PERFORMER	RECORD TITLE	AUTHOR	RECORD LABEL
Robert Frost	*Robert Frost in Recital*	Robert Frost	Caed TC 1523
Marianne Moore	*Marianne Moore Reads Her Poetry*	Marianne Moore	CMS 678
Sylvia Plath	*Sylvia Plath Reading Her Poetry*	Sylvia Plath	Caed TC 1544
Dylan Thomas	*A Child's Christmas in Wales*	Dylan Thomas	Caed TC 1002
Herbert Morrison	*The Last Flight of the Hindenburg*	Radio Broadcast	Mark 56 656
Churchill, Roosevelt, Hitler, Mussolini, and others	*Into the Storm —The Coming of the War, 1939*	BBC Archives	CMS 112
George Irving	*The Tongue Twisters*		Caed TC 1432

Speech Science

Bell Telephone Laboratories	*The Science of Sound*		Folk 6007

Foreign Language Records

PERFORMER	RECORD TITLE	AUTHOR	RECORD LABEL
La Comédie Française	*Le Bourgeois Gentilhomme*	Molière	Sp Arts 794
	Le Malade Imaginaire	Molière	Sp Arts 794

Accents and Dialects

ACCENT OR DIALECT	TITLE	AUTHOR	LABEL
Southern Speech and others	*The Art of Ruth Draper*		Sp Arts RD5, 779, 798/800
Southwestern Speech (Hal Holbrook)	*Mark Twain Tonight*	Mark Twain	COL OS 2019
Cultivated British (Noel Coward and Margaret Leighton)	*Duologues*		Caed TC 1069
Cockney	*Major Barbara*	G. B. Shaw	Caed TRS 319
Irish (Siobhan McKenna)	*Irish Folk Tales*		Sp Arts 720

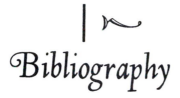

Bibliography

Dialects

Machlin, Evangeline. *Dialects for the Stage: A Manual and Two Cassette Tapes.* New York: Theatre Art Books, 1975.

Anthologies of Poetry
Useful for Practicing Speech Techniques

Allison, Alexander W. et al, eds. *The Norton Anthology of Poetry: Shorter Edition.* New York: W. W. Norton & Co., 1970.

Bernikow, Louise, ed. *The World Split Open: Four Centuries of Women Poets in England and America, 1552-1950.* New York: Random House (Vintage Books), 1974.

Creekmore, Hubert, ed. *A Little Treasury of World Poetry.* New York: Charles Scribners' Sons, 1952.

Hine, Daryl, and Parisi, Joseph, eds. *The Poetry Anthology: 1912-1977.* Boston: Houghton Mifflin Co., 1978.

Lomax, A., and Abdul, R., eds. *Three Thousand Years of Black Poetry.* Greenwich, Conn.: Fawcett Publications, 1970.

Swallow, Alan, ed. *The Rinehart Book of Verse.* New York: Holt, Rinehart & Winston, 1964.

Untermeyer, Louis, ed. *Rainbow in the Sky.* New York: Harcourt, Brace & Co., 1935. (A valuable book for reading aloud to children.)

Phonetic Dictionaries

Jones, Daniel. *A Pronouncing Dictionary on Phonetic Principles.* New York: E. P. Dutton, 1963.

Kenyon, John S., and Knott, Thomas A. *A Pronouncing Dictionary of American English.* Springfield, Mass.: G & C Merriam Co., 1953.

Appendix A

EXERCISES FOR THE CORRECTION OF FAULTS IN SPEECH TONE

Exercises for the Correction of Stridency

Preparation

Make a one -minute recording of your voice, putting on it the date on which you begin daily practice of these exercises. Discuss informally on your recording the problem of your strident tone in relation to your acting. End with a reading of your choice—poetry, prose, or drama. Preserve this recording. (The practice recordings you make as part of the exercises below need not be preserved for more than a month, as suggested.)

Correction

GROUP A. LISTENING TO IDENTIFY STRIDENCY

1. Carry a diary with you, and make memoranda of any high, tense, nagging, or belligerent voices you may hear. Note the age and sex of the speaker and the circumstances. Comment on the effect upon you of the high pitch and loud tone.

2. Listen to documentary recordings, such as *Into the Storm—The Coming of the War, 1939* (CMS 112), and to recordings of authors reading their own works. Identify stridency when you hear it by its hard, loud, unvaried quality. Collect on tape samples of strident voices for reference.

3. Listen to stridency used for dramatic effect, as by Uta Hagen in the record of *Who's Afraid of Virginia Woolf?* (Columbia, DOL287). Note the impression of violent emotion which strident tone evokes.

GROUP B. EXERCISES FOR REPLACING STRIDENCY WITH RELAXED TONE

1. *Achieving Deep Relaxation.* Complete steps 1 through 8 in the first series of relaxation exercises in Chapter 5. Continue with the following steps:

    a. Inhale deeply. Yawn with a long, sighing exhalation. Rest a moment. If the impulse to yawn occurs, obey it, and yawn as fully as you can. Continue yawning for several minutes, spontaneously, or with yawns induced by opening the mouth very wide as you inhale and exhale deeply and slowly.

    b. Yawn as before, but on the exhalation, vocalize very gently, with a steady slide down in pitch:

Uh
                              uh

    c. Rise, as described in the relaxation exercises, Chapter 5. Undertake the transition series of exercises, ending with head rolling and prolonged yawning.

    d. Do one or more of the breath control exercises from Chapter 6, Group B.

    e. Do the humming, singing, and speaking exercises in Chapter 7, Group B. Keep your pitch low.

2. *Practicing with Relaxed Tone in a Six-Month Series.* Daily, after finishing the preliminary exercises, read aloud one of the selections below or a poem similar in mood. Read sitting down, leaning back, well relaxed. Read quietly, but do not use an unvarying low pitch. Rather use meaningful inflections, simply keeping the tone relaxed. Read it several times, until your reading feels easy and natural. Then make a dated recording of the selection. Each day for the month following, add another dated recording of the same selection, made directly after you finished the preliminary exercises. At the end of the

month, listen to the entire set of recordings of the same stanza, and note your progress towards unforced, resonant tone.

During the next five months, make five similar series. Use a selection from those below or a similar poem of your choice for each series.

Continue each day with Units 5 and 6 of the Actor's Practice Routine described at the end of this book. At this time, omit Units 7 and 8.

So smooth, so sweet, so sil'vry is thy voice,
As, could they hear, the Damned would make no noise,
But listen to thee, (walking in thy chamber,)
Melting melodious words to Lutes of Amber.
ROBERT HERRICK, *Upon Julia's Voice*

They have no song, the sedges dry,
  And still they sing,
It is within my breast they sing,
  As I pass by.
Within my breast they touch a string,
  They wake a sigh,
There is but sound of sedges dry,
  In me they sing.
GEORGE MEREDITH, *Song of the Songless*

It is morning, I awake from a bed of silence,
Shining I rise from the starless waters of sleep.
The walls are about me still as in the evening,
I am the same, and the same name still I keep.
The earth revolves with me, yet makes no motion,
The stars pale silently in a coral sky.
In a whistling void I stand before my mirror,
Unconcerned, and tie my tie.
CONRAD AIKEN, Morning Song from *"Senlin"*

As a white candle
In a holy place,
So is the beauty
Of an agèd face.

As the spent radiance
Of a winter sun,
So is a woman
With her travail done.

Her brood gone from her,
And her thoughts as still
As the waters
Under a ruined mill.

JOSEPH CAMPBELL, The Old Woman

Slow, slow, fresh fount, keep time with my salt tears,
    Yet slower yet, oh, faintly, gentle springs.
List to the heavy part the music bears,
    Woe weeps out her division when she sings.
        Droop, herbs and flowers,
        Fall grief in showers,
        Our beauties are not ours.
          Oh, I could still
Like melting snow upon some craggy hill,
    Drop, drop, drop, drop,
Since Nature's pride is now a withered daffodil.

BEN JONSON, Echo's Lament for Narcissus

I am swimming to a dark island,
An island covered with cypress,
Long veils and pale garlands
Of moss brush my face as I pass
        through the still water.

I am swimming through the dark water,
The island now rises above me,
The water is warm, the feeling is softer
Than wind as mists in the valley
        curl around cypress.

I am standing in groves of dark cypress.
The island lies all around me
In silence. I move through the stillness
To look back toward the land hid by the sea
        from the dark island.

GABRIELLE LADD, The Dark Island

Confirmation

At the end of six months, or whenever you feel you have
achieved habitual relaxed and resonant tone, make a second
conversational recording, directly following the one made in
preparation for the corrective work. Compare the two, and

judge whether your strident tone is now replaced by relaxed tone. If not, continue until this is achieved.

Exercises for the Correction of Hoarseness

Preparation

Make a dated recording of yourself in conversation with a teacher or friend whose vocal tone is clear. Discuss any subject of mutual interest, so that your speech may be as nearly as possible as it is when you are unconscious of it. Listen to the recording, and estimate the degree of hoarseness in your tone by comparing it with the clear voice. Preserve this recording. (Recordings made as part of the exercises below need not be preserved.)

Correction

GROUP A. LISTENING TO IDENTIFY HOARSENESS

1. Marked hoarseness is rarely heard on records you can buy. However, listen for traces of it in the recordings by older writers of their own works, such as William Faulkner and Robert Frost, and in documentaries such as *Into the Storm— The Coming of the War, 1939* (CMS 112). Collect on tape samples of such voices for reference.

2. Observe the onset of hoarseness in actors who continue to rehearse and perform with sore throats. Note the rapid deterioration of the speech tone.

3. Listen to the deliberate assumption of hoarseness for dramatic effect by Jason Robards in the record *Excerpts from Eugene O'Neill* (Columbia, OL5900). Note the unpleasant effect even of controlled hoarseness.

GROUP B. EXERCISES FOR REPLACING HOARSE TONE
WITH CLEAR TONE

1. *Achieving Deep Relaxation.* Follow the program for achieving deep relaxation described under Exercises for the Correction of Stridency, Group B, Exercise 1. In *(e)* of Exercise 1, work at the pitch level, whether high or low, at which you can sing or speak with the greatest comfort and clearest tone. Record yourself in these exercises. Listen to the recording, and select one or two key syllables in which your tone is clearest. The exercises which follow are based on the assumption that these syllables may be *mah*, and *mow*, (as in "mound"). If these are not your key syllables, substitute those that are. Work lying down, sitting or standing, depending on which position allows you to speak with the greatest relaxation.

In undertaking this, and in succeeding exercises, use extreme caution to avoid fatiguing your voice. Pause and rest your voice after each five minutes of work. For the first two months practice for only two or three five-minute periods in all. Thereafter, lengthen your practice period in accordance with your ability to produce clear tone without fatigue.

> *a.* Repeat the following syllables six times each, very softly and slowly. You should just cross the threshold from whispered speech to phonation. Record yourself, and listen to the clarity of your tone.
>
> Mow . . . mow . . . mow . . . mow . . . mow . . . mow
> Mah . . . mah . . . mah . . . mah . . . mah . . . mah
>
> *b.* Repeat (*a*), very gradually increasing the loudness of your tone through the six repetitions. The last syllable should be as loud as ordinary conversational tone. Record the exercise, checking on the clarity of the last, loudest syllables especially.
>
> *c.* Speak the following word-and-phrase pairs softly and slowly, with the clearest tone you can produce. Sus-

tain the vowels on the single words, using speech which is just short of intoning. Try to match the tone of the vowels in the phrases to that of the vowels in the words. Invent similar words and phrases, if necessary, around your own key vowels.

(1) ARMS
Arms and the man.

FARM
Rich farmlands dark as coal.

HARBOR
Going down to Bar Harbor.

CALM
The calm before a storm.

ARGUE
Arguing over a point of law.

SNARL
A snarled coil of wire.

HARM
Secure and free from harm.

LARGO
Listening to Handel's *Largo.*

MARNE
The battle of the Marne in World War I.

FARCE
Laughing heartily at a rousing farce.

(2) DOWN
Down in the valley below.

TOWN
Going downtown now.

LOUD
The loud sound of the bells.

BOUGHS
Under the boughs of the deep forest.

POWER
A downfall from absolute power.

EXPOUND
Expounding dogmas of ancient religions.

HOUSE
House of Lords and House of Commons

MOUNTAIN
Three mountain-tops, three silent pinnacles of
agèd snow.
TENNYSON

SCOUNDREL
He said "I am a scoundrel," and felt profoundly
satisfied.
VICTOR HUGO

BOUNTY
My bounty is as boundless as the sea,
My love as great, for both are infinite.
SHAKESPEARE

3. *Producing Clear Tone With Various Adjustments on the Same Line.* Read the following lines six times, making the adjustments described below. Work for slowly increasing clarity of tone. As soon as you can read the line with six variations, record yourself doing the sequence of six. Play it back to check

your success in improving the tone. Repeat the exercise daily with any other unit of poetry of about the same length.

> Thou, silent form, dost tease us out of thought
> As doth eternity.
>
> JOHN KEATS, *Ode on a Grecian Urn*

a. Read the sentence silently, carefully shaping all the sounds, but not using the vocal cords.
b. Read the sentence as softly as possible.
c. Inhale deeply, and read it holding the vowel in "Thou" for one or two seconds.
d. Read it, firmly shaping and prolonging the *l, m,* and *n* sounds.
e. Read it raising your pitch markedly on "tease" and prolonging the vowel.
f. Read it to communicate, trying to include the adjustments you made for *(c), (d),* and *(e).*

4. *Producing Clear Tone in a Six-Month Series.* Do Exercise 2, Group B, for the correction of stridency. Aim chiefly at the production of clear, soft tone. Sustain especially your key vowels, which you should underline wherever they occur in the selections. Gradually increase the loudness of your tone as your ability to maintain clarity on all vowels and diphthongs increases.

Continue each day's work with Units 5 and 6 of the Actor's Practice Routine.

Confirmation

At the end of each three months, during one year of the corrective work, make successive conversational recordings directly following your first one. Compare each with the one preceding it, and judge whether your hoarseness is being replaced by clear tone. Continue the corrective work until this goal is achieved.

Exercises for the Correction
of Nasality

Preparation

Make a dated recording of yourself in conversation with a teacher or friend whose vocal tone is free from nasality. Discuss any subject of mutual interest, so that your speech may be as nearly as possible as it is when you are unconscious of it. Listen to the recording, and estimate the degree of nasality you now have. Preserve this recording. (The practice recordings you make as part of the exercises below need not be preserved.)

Correction

GROUP A.   LISTENING TO IDENTIFY NASALITY

1. Read aloud the limerick below, deliberately using a nasal twang on the vowel in any *one of* the italicized words. As you say the others, open your mouth wide to avoid nasalizing their vowels. Record yourself reading the limerick several times, with random use of nasality on one of these words each time. Play back your recording, and identify the nasalized syllables. Listen with closed eyes, to help you concentrate on the quality of the vowel tone.

> There was a young *man* who said "*Why*
> *Can't* I look in my *ear* with my *eye?*
>   If I give my *mind* to it,
>   I'm sure I *can* do it.
> You never *can* tell till you *try.*"
>
> ANONYMOUS

2. Repeat each of the words in the list below four times, the first time with the mouth open wide. This helps to prevent nasalization of vowels by making it hard for the soft palate to

remain lowered. (See Figure 6.) On the fourth repetition, deliberately nasalize the vowel, opening the mouth as little as possible. Record the exercise, and check on whether it was carried out correctly.

man	men	minnow
sand	send	sinned
Dan	den	din
tang	tongue	ting
ham	hem	him
time	dine	mine
now	town	found

3. Repeat Exercise 2, but nasalize the vowel once at random during the four repetitions. Record the exercise, listen to it, and identify each nasalized vowel.

4. Read and record the word-list in threes, going across the page. Nasalize any one vowel each time. Listen and identify it as before.

5. Find the nasal voice on the documentary record *Hearings of the Un-American Activities Committee,* San Francisco (Folkways 5530).

GROUP B. EXERCISES FOR REPLACING NASALITY
WITH CLEAR TONE

1. *Correcting Nasality on Single Words*
   a. Read the word list above, opening your mouth more widely than usual on the vowel sounds. Go slowly, avoiding any trace of nasality, feeling the vowels resound in your mouth. Record your reading, and listen to it to check on its freedom from nasality.
   b. Pronounce the word "now" very slowly, breaking the diphthong *ow* into its two elements, *ah* and *oo*. Open the mouth wide for the *ah* and sustain it. Glide slowly to the *oo*:

   Nah . . . oo, nah . . . oo, nah . . . oo

   Repeat, gliding rapidly from ah to oo:

Nah-oo, nah-oo, nah-oo

Repeat, sounding the diphthong as one unit:

Now, now, now

Opening your mouth wide at the start of *ow*, read the following lines of Shakespeare in full voice:

Now is the winter of our discontent
Made glorious summer by this sun of York.

Now are our brows bound with victorious wreaths.
Our bruised arms hung up for monuments.

Now entertain conjecture of a time
When creeping murmur and the pouring dark
Fills the wide vessel of the universe.

Now all the youth of England is on fire,
For *now* sits Expectation in the air.

Now attest
That those whom you call fathers did beget you.

2. *Correcting Nasality by Strengthening the Soft Palate.* This exercise strengthens the soft palate by lowering and raising it repeatedly in the sound sequences below.

    a. Repeat the following pair of sounds often. Feel the soft palate lowering for the *ng*.

Ng . . . ah, ng . . . ah, ng . . . ah

    b. Repeat the exercise soundlessly, with eyes closed. You will clearly feel the downward pull of the soft palate for the *ng*.

    c. Repeat the exercise for one minute twice a day for several weeks. Vary it with the combinations below.

Ng . . . oh, ng . . . aw, ng . . . ow, ng . . . ay, ng . . . eye

3. *Correcting Nasality in Sentences without Nasal Consonants.* Say each of the sentences twice, holding your nose the first time, letting it go the second. Record them, and listen to find out if both repetitions of the sentence are free from nasality. The first should be so because you have blocked off the nose from outside, with your fingers, the second because you have blocked it off from inside, by keeping the soft palate raised.

> Say your vowels carefully always.
> Keep your lips apart as you do so.
> Feel exactly where vowels occur.
> They always should be wholly oral.
> Read poetry aloud for good vowel quality.
> As you do so, watch each stressed word.
> Ask yourself, "Is it spelled with a short vowel?"
> If it is, part your lips as you speak it.
> Use this lips-apart approach for all your vowels.
> Keep your ears alert so that you catch a vowel error
> just as it occurs.

4. *Correcting Nasality in Continuous Reading.* Read aloud the passage below from the book of Ecclesiastes in the Old Testament. Avoid any nasality, especially on the word *time.*

> For everything there is a season,
>   and a time for every matter under heaven:
> a time to be born, and a time to die;
> a time to plant, and a time to pluck up what is planted;
> a time to kill and a time to heal;
> a time to break down, and a time to build up;
> a time to weep, and a time to laugh;
> a time to mourn, and a time to dance;
> a time to cast away stones, and a time to gather stones
>   together;
> a time to keep silence, and a time to speak;
> a time to love, and a time to hate;
> a time for war, and a time for peace.
>   What gain has the worker from his toil?
>   Ecclesiastes, Chapter 3

5. *Correcting Nasality in a Six-Month Series.* For six months, read aloud your own selections of poetry or prose each day,

recording them and checking to see that your speech tone is free from nasality throughout. Continue daily with Units 5, 6, 7, and 8 of the Actor's Practice Routine.

Confirmation

At the end of six months, or whenever you feel you have achieved speech tone habitually free from nasality, make a second conversational recording, directly after the first. Compare the two, and judge whether you have reached your goal or not. If not, continue the corrective exercises until it is achieved.

Exercises for the Correction of Breathiness

Preparation

Make a dated recording of yourself in conversation with a teacher or friend whose vocal tone is free from breathiness. Discuss any subject of mutual interest, so that your speech may be as nearly as possible as it is when you are unconscious of it. Listen to the recording and estimate the degree of breathiness you now have. Preserve the recording. (The practice recordings you make as part of the exercises below need not be preserved.)

Correction

GROUP A. LISTENING TO IDENTIFY BREATHINESS

1. Practice the word list as shown below, saying each word three times clearly, the fourth time deliberately blowing out a puff of air before the vowel. Listen closely to the quality of breathiness as you hear yourself make it in the fourth repetition.

pipe	pipe	pipe	pʰipe
pike	pike	pike	pʰike
type	type	type	tʰype
tile	tile	tile	tʰile
kite	kite	kite	kʰite
kind	kind	kind	kʰind

2. Repeat Exercise 1, but speak the breathy syllable sometimes first, sometimes second, third, or fourth in the series of four repetitions. Keep the puff of breath strong. Record yourself doing the exercise, continuing the random utterance of one breathy syllable during each four. Listen to your recording, and identify the breathy syllable whenever it occurs.

3. Repeat Exercise 2, using the slightest possible puff on the breathy syllable.

4. Read aloud the limerick below, using a breathy tone on *either* "bright," "light," or "night." Record yourself reading it several times, with random use of breathiness on one of these words each time. Play back your recording, and identify the breathy quality wherever it occurs.

RELATIVITY

There was a young lady called *Bright*
Who could travel much faster than *light*.
She started one day
In the relative way,
And came back the previous *night*.

ANONYMOUS

5. Listen to deliberately breathy speech, used as a stage whisper for dramatic effect, by Albert Finney as Romeo, in the recorded *Romeo and Juliet*, II, i, (Caedmon, SRSM228). Listen also to the sighing breathiness of "O esperance!" as spoken by Michael Redgrave as Hotspur in *Henry IV*, Part I, II, iii. (*Soul of an Age*, Caedmon, TC1170). Note that the actor can sometimes turn what is normally a fault into a dramatic device.

GROUP B. EXERCISES FOR REPLACING BREATHY TONE
WITH RESONANT TONE

1. *Correcting Breathy Tone by Replacing It with Singing Tone.* Singing tone is produced when the vocal cords are brought close together as the tone is produced. Pure singing tone cannot be breathy.

Sing each of the following on a comfortable middle pitch, holding the vowel. Then intone it briefly. Then speak it, briefly but musically. Start the vowel tone immediately after the consonant.

Sing	Intone	Speak
pi........ne	pi....ne	pine
ti.........ne	ti....ne	tine
ki.......nd	ki....nd	kind
mi.......ne	mi....ne	mine
si.........gn	si....gn	sign
fi.........ne	fi....ne	fine

2. *Correcting Breathy Tone by Lengthening Vowels.* Read the following stanzas aloud, lengthening the italicized vowels. Be sure that each vowel begins directly after its preceding consonant. Record yourself, and listen to your recording to check on this.

Aw*a*ke! for morning in the B*ow*l of Night
Has flung the St*o*ne that puts the St*a*rs to flight,
    And lo! the Hunter of the East has c*au*ght
The Sultan's Turret in a N*oo*se of Light.

And when the Sun rose, those who st*oo*d before
The T*a*vern, shouted "*O*pen then the d*oo*r!
    You kn*ow* how little while we have to st*a*y,
And once departed, may return no more.

Edward Fitzgerald, from *The Rubaiyat of Omar Khayyam*

3. *Correcting Breathy Tone in a Six-Month Series.* For six months, read aloud daily several stanzas from *The Rubaiyat of*

Omar Khayyam, lengthening the vowels when appropriate to the metre and the meaning as in the preceding exercise. Record yourself each time, checking to see that you make no breathy vowels. Continue each day with Units 5, 6, 7, and 8 of the Actor's Practice Routine.

Confirmation

At the end of six months, or whenever you feel you have achieved speech tone habitually free from breathiness, make a second conversational recording, directly after the first. Compare the two, and judge whether you have reached your goal or not. If not, continue the corrective exercises until it is achieved.

Appendix B

The Actor's Daily Routine: A Long-range Approach

The series of exercises set out below provides an alternative to that given on the first end pages. By now you are familiar with all the material in this book, and can use it as suggested in each practice unit. Throughout your professional life, spend at least fifteen minutes twice a day on your practice, working systematically through the exercise units. Plan to practice at the same time and in the same place each day, working where you may speak as loudly as necessary to strengthen your voice.

Vary your practice with materials of your own choice from poetry, prose, or drama. Since you are developing speech skills, not acting skills, do not work on the lines of a role which you are rehearsing for a performance. The purpose of your practice is to make all the techniques of good speech so habitual that they are immediately available to your performance needs.

Unit 1. Relaxation

Carry out a full relaxation routine, lying down, sitting or standing, as described in Chapter 5.

Unit 2. Transition Exercises

Do three or more of the transition exercises in Chapter 5. You may substitute for these any free-moving exercises you may have learned in dance or gymnastic work.

Unit 3. Breath Control

Do at least one exercise from each of Groups B, C, D, E, and F, under Breath Control in Chapter 6. Choose different ones each day. Invent new similar ones of your own for variety.

Unit 4. Resonance

Do selected exercises from Groups B and C under Resonance in Chapter 7. If you have one of the speech tone faults described in that chapter, substitute the appropriate exercise group in the Appendix, until the fault is corrected.

Unit 5. Articulation

Do one or two exercises daily from each of Groups A and B, in Chapter 8 on agility of articulation and accuracy of articulation. Use different exercises each day.

Unit 6. Variety

Do one or two exercises daily from each of the exercise groups B, C, and D in Chapter 9 for developing variety of pitch, rate, and stress. Complete this unit with the reading of a poem or prose passage from this book or of your own choice, applying to it these three techniques of variety.

Unit 7. Ear-Training

Listen to an actor's recorded speech in a play or recording. Records of outstanding Shakespearean productions are good choices. Transcribe five to ten lines each day both in phonetic transcription and in pitch transcription on music paper, as described in Chapter 7. Read aloud daily the lines you transcribed the previous day. Record yourself in so doing and compare your recording with the original. The two should substantially match in pronunciation and in inflection patterns. If they do, your transcriptions were correct.

Unit 8. Sight-Reading and Projection

Freely read at sight a speech from a play with which you are not familiar. Enter into the meaning of the lines whole-heartedly, forgetting speech techniques. Move about as you read if you wish. Project your speech naturally, as described in Chapter 3.

On occasion, when you feel you have both caught the spirit of the lines and are expressing them with all the speech techniques at your command, record your reading, dating it. Listen to it a month later and appraise its success.

The Actor's Warm-up Exercises

THE FOLLOWING is a series of simple exercises which you may use as a five-minute warm-up for your speech, so that you may rehearse or perform without strain. Repeat each exercise five to ten times.

1. *Preparation.* Feet apart, stretch up tall. Bend from the waist, loosely but vigorously. Try to sag the fingers to the floor. Raise the trunk, stand erect, and swing arms in large circles, one at a time.

2. *Relaxation.* Yawn, inhaling deeply and stretching the jaw as wide open as possible. Vocalize as you exhale, *aaaaah!*

3. *Breath Control.* Breath in deeply and fully. Exhale as slowly as possible through rounded lips.

4. *Humming.* Starting at a low pitch easy for you, hum one octave up the scale slowly, four prolonged *m's* to each breath.

5. *Singing.* Sing with wide-open mouth, on a do-me-sol-do-sol-mi-do tune (C-E-G-C-G-E-C),

<pre>
                    mah
              mah   mah
          mah   mah
      mah   mah
</pre>

Repeat, starting one tone higher each time. Vary the exercise by using *moh, maw,* or *mee* instead of *mah.*

6. *Intoning.* Repeat the above exercise, intoning the syllables and keeping the speech pitch at or near the sung tone.

7. *Resonating*
   a. Say the phrases below loudly, one to a breath, lengthening the italized vowels.

D*ow*n and *Ou*t	H*e*re tod*ay*
N*ow* and Then	G*o*ne tom*o*rrow
Who are *you*	A l*ou*d s*ou*nd
M*e* and m*i*ne	A r*ou*nd t*o*ne
F*a*r aw*ay*	Hold your v*ow*els

   b. Repeat the following, lengthening the italicized words.

   The *moon* on the *one* hand, the *sun* on the other.
   The *moon* is my sister, the *sun* is my brother.
   The *moon* on the left hand, the *sun* on the right,
   My brother, good *morning; my* sister, good *night.*

8. *Articulating.* Say the following limerick, or any that you know by heart, in less than 10 seconds. Keep the consonants sharp.

A tutor who tooted the flute
Tried to tutor two tutors to toot.
Said the two to the tutor
Is it harder to toot, or
To tutor two tooters to toot?

9. *Projecting.* Say the following or any similar group of lines in full voice, with lengthened vowels, lengthened *m*'s, *n*'s, and *ng*'s, and with well-opened mouth.

Now entertain conjecture of a time
When creeping murmur and the pouring dark
Fills the wide vessel of the universe!

10. *Interpreting.* Use the following, or any speech from a current role of yours, to complete the warmup. Say it in full voice, and with clear emphasis where needed.

SONNET XXIII

As an unperfect actor on the stage,
Who with his fear is put beside his part,
Or some fierce thing replete with too much rage,
Whose strength's abundance weakens his own heart,
So I, for fear of trust, forget to say
The perfect ceremony of love's rite,
And in mine own love's strength seem to decay,
O'ercharged with burden of mine own love's might.
O let my looks be then the eloquence
And dumb presagers of my speaking breast,
Who plead for love, and look for recompense
More than that tongue that more hath more expressed.
   O learn to read what silent love hath writ;
   To hear with eyes belongs to love's fine wit.

SHAKESPEARE

Appendix C

ADVANCED EXERCISES IN SPEECH TECHNIQUES

Exercises for Speech Techniques in Combination: Projection, Breath Control, Resonance, Articulation, Variety

As you read aloud the exercises and poems below, think about applying first one technique, then the other, then both, to your speech while speaking the lines. Provide yourself also with an anthology of modern poetry, either one of your own choice or one of those in the Bibliography on page 221.

1. *For Projection and Resonance*
   a. Begin by sounding out pure resonant vowels of some duration. Then cut them up and contour them with the consonants. Think of setting up the stream of breath, the stream of sound, and the stream of speech as a sequence. Think of the *moving* parts of the mouth—the jaw, tongue, lips, soft palate.

   Sounding vowels with consonants:

   ```
   ah.........ha..........pa
   ee.........me.........we
   oh.........no.........woe
   I..........my.........why
   oo.........do.........who
   ow........how........now
   oy.........joy.........boy
   you.......music.......beauty
   ```

b. Use "how" as a tone-maker. Prolong it in the phrases below. Open your mouth well. Inhale gently at need.

How nice! How are you? How much? How about that? How are things? How've you been? How d'you know?

c. Speak the following in full voice, like an inspired visionary. Ring out every long vowel, and every nasal, *m*, *n*, and *ng*.

I VISION GOD
(A Folk-Sermon)

I vision God standing
On the heights of Heaven,
Throwing the devil like
A burning torch
Over the gulf
Into the valleys of hell.
His eye the lightning's flash,
His voice the thunder's roll.
With one hand He snatched
The sun from its socket,
And the other He clapped across the moon.

I vision God wringing
A storm from the heavens;
Rocking the world
Like an earthquake;
Blazing the sea
With a trail of fire.
His eye the lightning's flash,
His voice the thunder's roll,
With one hand He snatched
The sun from its socket,
And the other He clapped across the moon.

I vision God standing
On a mountain
Of burnished gold,
Blowing His breath
Of silver clouds
Over the world.

His eye the lightning's flash,
His voice the thunder's roll.
With one hand He snatched
The sun from its socket,
And the other He clapped across the moon.

From Z. N. HURSTON, *Jonah's Gourd Vine*

2. *For Breath Control and Resonance*

a. Use the following sequence as you practice the poems below.
   (1) Read the poem aloud at sight.
   (2) In a mirror, watch your breathing, keeping it low and full.
   (3) Sit, and read the poem. Feel with the finger tips the resonance in five hollows — throat, mouth, parted lips, nasal bone and skull.
   (4) Read the poem again, lengthening the vowels, diphthongs, and voiced consonants.
   (5) Gradually let the meaning guide the reading.
   (6) Practice from memory, watching that the breathing is low, resonance full, and communication active.

b. Keeping relaxed, read this stanza in two breaths, one taken at the beginning and one after "bright."

I saw Eternity the other night,
Like a great *Ring* of pure and endless light,
All calm, as it was bright,
And round beneath it, Time, in hours, days, years,
Driv'n by the spheres,
Like a vast shadow moved; in which the world
And all her train, were hurled.

HENRY VAUGHAN, *The World*

c. When you have reached (6) under (a) above, practice the following sonnet using one breath to four lines for the first twelve lines, then one breath for the closing couplet. Use vivid, free-ranging inflections.

SONNET 29

When in disgrace with Fortune and men's eyes,
I all alone beweep my outcast state,
And trouble deaf Heaven with my bootless cries,
And look upon myself, and curse my fate,

Wishing me like to one more rich in hope,
Featur'd like him, like him with friends possess'd,
Desiring this man's art, and that man's scope,
With what I most enjoy contented least;

Yet in these thoughts myself almost despising,
Haply I think on thee—and then my state
(Like to the lark at break of day arising
From sullen earth) sings hymns at heaven's gate;

For thy sweet love remember'd such wealth brings,
That then I scorn to change my state with kings.

WILLIAM SHAKESPEARE

d. Find other sonnets that appeal to you. Practice them in the same way.

3. *For Articulation and Variety.* Pronounce the following verses in three ways:

—With strongly made, exaggerated lip shapes and tongue movements.

—With moderate but vigorous lip shapes and tongue movements.

—With slack, minimal lip shapes and tongue movements.

Monitor the results first by ear, then by recording your practice. Observe the differences between your three readings.

—Forgetting articulation, practice the verses for variety, exaggerating as you think appropriate.

a. Limericks:

THE COMMENT
There once was a man who said "God
Must think it exceedingly odd
   If He finds that this tree
   Continues to be,
When there's no one about in the quad."[1]

THE RESPONSE
"Dear Sir,
   Your astonishment's odd.
I am always about in the quad,
   And that's why the tree
   Will continue to be,
Since observed by
        Yours faithfully,
          God."

ANONYMOUS

b. One-liners:
These are made up of famous first lines and irreverent second lines. Read them with earnest commitment on each first line, then shift completely and read the second line deadpan, or in mock-serious, ironic, or comic style, or whatever seems appropriate to you.

The second lines are by the author. For fun, write some more for yourself to follow other famous first lines. Try them on an audience.

In Xanadu did Kubla Khan
Team up with OPEC and Iran.

Awake! for Morning in the Bowl of Night
Has mixed some lumpy oatmeal, out of spite.

Is this the face that launched a thousand ships?
Think of the problems with those radar blips!

When I see birches lean to left and right,
I wish they'd fall. My stove'd burn all night!

1 quad: a rectangle of lawn bounded by four college buildings.

There is a singer everyone has heard,
Some of us wish the pleasure'd been deferred.

When in disgrace with Fortune and men's eyes,
I start right in and bake some apple pies.

O that this too too solid flesh would melt![2]
I'd love to take some inches off my belt.

     c. A poem to say in 60 seconds, then in 50, then, if you
can, in 45. Blend into one the two *n*'s of "and n . . ."
in "hundred 'n' ninety."

In Fourteen Hundred and Ninety-Two
Columbus sailed the ocean blue,
And it's just as well, I beg to state,
That it wasn't in 1498;
Though had it been, I might erect
A rhyme in Daly dialect, [3]
Like "In Fourteen Hond'ed an' Ninety-Eight
Colombo sail for Unita State."
But the year wouldn't matter a little bit
To a narrative poet, viz., to wit:
In Fourteen Hundred and Ninety-One
Columbus sailed for the setting sun;
Or in Fourteen Hundred and Ninety-Three
Columbus sailed the bright blue sea;
Or in Fourteen Hundred and Ninety-Four
Columbus sailed for San Salvador;
Or in Fourteen Hundred and Ninety-Five
Columbus sailed for the Western Hive
(A Western Hive is nothing whatever,
But in narrative verse it sounds pretty clever);
     Or in Fourteen Hundred and Ninety-Six
     Columbus did some juggling tricks;
     Or in Fourteen Hundred and Ninety-Seven
     Columbus discovered the Land of Heaven;

[2] Sources for first lines are Samuel Coleridge, *Kubla Khan;* Edward
Fitzgerald, *The Rubaiyat of Omar Khayyam;* Christopher Marlowe, *The
Tragical History of Dr. Faustus;* Robert Frost, *Birches;* Robert Frost, *The
Ovenbird;* William Shakespeare, *Sonnet 29;* William Shakespeare, *Hamlet.*

[3] T. A. Daly wrote verse in exaggerated Italian dialect.

Or in Fourteen Hundred and Ninety-Nine
Columbus sailed the wavy brine.
Columbus, then, in whatever year,
Discovered the Western Hemisphere . . .

FRANKLIN P. ADAMS
(From *Christopher Columbus,* dedicated to
Stephen Vincent Benét, the gifted author of
John Brown's Body.)

4. *For Relaxation and Variety.* Read both the following in relaxed, conversational style. Treat the first with sophistication, the second, naïvely.

From BEGINNING MY STUDIES

Beginning my studies, the first step pleased me so much,
The mere fact consciousness, these forms, the power of motion,
The least insect or animal, the senses, eyesight, love,
The first step, I say, awed me and pleased me so much,
I have hardly gone and hardly wished to go any farther,
But stop and loiter all the time and sing it in ecstatic songs.

WALT WHITMAN

MY MOTHER IS A GOOD MOTHER

My mother is a good mother and I love her very much.
And she cooks very good. Most of the time I stay
in the house and watch her cook. She is a good
housewife and when I want money she gives it to me.

When I wake up in the morning she kisses me,
And when I go to sleep at night. And every time
I see a pretty girl walking down the street,
my mother slaps me.

But I tricked the hell out of her one day.
I said "Mom, the chicken's burning!" Mom went in
the house, and I said to that girl, "Hi, baby!
Do you want me to walk with you down the street?"
Then she said, "Hell, no!"

MIKE ODOMS (aged eleven)
in *Young Voices From the Black Ghetto*

5. *For All Techniques.* The following poem is full of music. Read it with special attention to the glides, *l*, *w*, and *r*.

BINSEY POPLARS
felled 1879

My aspens dear, whose airy cages quelled,
Quelled or quenched in leaves the leaping sun,
All felled, felled, are all felled;
   Of a fresh and following folded rank
      Not spared, not one
      That dandled a sandalled
    Shadow that swam or sank
On meadow and river and wind-wandering weed-winding bank.

  O if we but knew what we do
     When we delve or hew—
    Hack and rack the growing green!
     Since country is so tender
    To touch, her being só slender,
    That, like this sleek and seeing ball
    But a prick will make no eye at all,
    Where we, even where we mean
      To mend her we end her,
     When we hew or delve:
After-comers cannot guess the beauty been.
  Ten or twelve, only ten or twelve
    Strokes of havoc únselve
     The sweet especial scene,
    Rural scene, a rural scene,
    Sweet especial rural scene.

GERARD MANLEY HOPKINS

Index

Printed in the United States
208580BV00003B/22-48/P